The Mongols in Iran

The polymath, Quṭb al-Dīn Shīrāzī, operated at the heart of the Ilkhanate state (1258–1335) from its inception under Hulegu. He worked alongside the scientist and political adviser, Nasir al-Dīn Ṭūsī, who had the ear of the Ilkhans and all their chief ministers.

The Mongols in Iran provides an annotated, paraphrased translation of a thirteenth-century historical chronicle penned, though not necessarily authored, by Quṭb al-Dīn Shīrāzī. This chronicle, a patchwork of anecdotes, detailed accounts, diary entries, and observations, comprises the notes and drafts of a larger, unknown, and probably lost historical work. It is specific, factual, and devoid of the rhetorical hyperbole and verbal arabesques so beloved of other writers of the period. It outlines the early years of the Chinggisid empire, recounts the rule of Hulegu Khan and his son Abaqa, and finally, details the travails and ultimate demise and death of Abaqa's brother and would-be successor, Ahmad Tegudar. Shirazi paints the Mongol khans in a positive light and opens his chronicle with a portrait of Chinggis Khan in almost hallowed terms.

Throwing new light on well-known personalities and events from the early Ilkhanate, this book will appeal to anyone studying the Mongol Empire, Mediaeval History, and Persian Literature.

George Lane returned to academia in 1991 after many years living and working in the Middle East and Asia. Since obtaining his PhD in 2001 he has published, lectured, and talked about the Mongols, the Ilkhanate, and various aspects of mediaeval Islamic history all over the world.

Routledge Studies in the History of Iran and Turkey
Edited by Carole Hillenbrand
University of Edinburgh

This series publishes important studies dealing with the history of Iran and Turkey in the period 1000–1700 AD. This period is significant because it heralds the advent of large numbers of nomadic Turks from Central Asia into the Islamic world. Their influence was felt particularly strongly in Iran and Turkey, territories which they permanently transformed.

The series presents translations of medieval Arabic and Persian texts which chronicle the history of the medieval Turks and Persians, and also publishes scholarly monographs which handle themes of medieval Turkish and Iranian history such as historiography, nomadisation and folk Islam.

The Rum Seljuqs
Evolution of a Dynasty
Songül Mecit

Turkic Peoples in Medieval Arabic Writings
Yehoshua Frenkel

Turkish Language, Literature and History
Travellers' Tales, Sultans and Scholars since the Eighth Century
Edited by Bill Hickman and Gary Leiser

Zengi and the Muslim Response to the Crusades
The Politics of Jihad
Taef Kamal El-Azhari

The Mongols in Iran
Quṭb Al-Dīn Shīrāzī's Akhbār-i Moghūlān
George Lane

For a full list of titles in the series, visit www.routledge.com/middleeaststudies/series/SE0697

The Mongols in Iran

Quṭb Al-Dīn Shīrāzī's Akhbār-i Moghūlān

George Lane

Routledge
Taylor & Francis Group
LONDON AND NEW YORK

First published 2018
by Routledge

2 Park Square, Milton Park, Abingdon, Oxfordshire OX14 4RN
52 Vanderbilt Avenue, New York, NY 10017

Routledge is an imprint of the Taylor & Francis Group, an informa business

First issued in paperback 2020

British Library Cataloguing-in-Publication Data
A catalogue record for this book is available from the British Library

Library of Congress Cataloging-in-Publication Data
Names: Lane, George, 1952– author.
Title: The Mongols in Iran : Quṭb Al-Dīn Shīrāzī's Akhbār-i Moghulān- / George Lane.
Other titles: Routledge studies in the history of Iran and Turkey.
Description: Milton Park, Abingdon, Oxon : Routledge, 2018. | Series: Routledge studies in the history of Iran and Turkey
Identifiers: LCCN 2018006779 | ISBN 9781138500525 (hbk) | ISBN 9781315143828 (ebk)
Subjects: LCSH: Quṭb al-Shīrāzī, Maḥmūd ibn Masᶜūd, 1236 or 1237–1310 or 1311—Criticism and interpretation. | Ilkhanid dynasty. | Iran—History—1256–1500. | Iran—Kings and rulers.
Classification: LCC DS289 .L37 2018 | DDC 955/.026—dc23
LC record available at https://lccn.loc.gov/2018006779

ISBN: 978-1-138-50052-5 (hbk)
ISBN: 978-0-367-60704-3 (pbk)

Typeset in Times New Roman
by Apex CoVantage, LLC

Contents

Preface

After centuries of gathering dust, lost in a large pile of disparate manuscripts, the late Iraj Afshar chanced upon this collection of historical notes penned though not necessarily authored by the polymath, Quṭb al-Dīn Shīrāzī. The jumbled pages of often scrawled script were hidden amongst other papers on a variety of subjects and by a variety of authors including the Jewish theosopher, Ibn Kammūna, his colleague Naṣīr al-Dīn Ṭūsī, the Islamic commentator, Shahrestānī, the poet, Sa'dī, and many other poets, thinkers, and writers from the mediaeval world. Iraj Afshar managed to sort the pages of historical observations and anecdotes into some kind of order and transcribe Shīrāzī's not easily decipherable script into an edited, legible text. His edited edition appeared in the holy city of Qum, central Iran, in 2009 along with the facsimile of the original and detailed notes and technical details about the original manuscripts including the order in which they had been found. From Afshar's notes it is clear that a number of pages have gone missing and that the manuscript as it stands was not a finished product. It seems more to have been a collection of notes and observations to aid later researchers and historians compile their histories and chronicles. Some of the folios from which Afshar worked were stamped with the seal of Rashīd al-Dīn's academy in Tabriz and indeed some of the incidents recorded in Shirazi's work appear verbatim in the *Jāma' al-Tavārīkh.*

Unfortunately, a great deal of the material from the great libraries of mediaeval Iran has been lost over the years as Persian capitals moved, were attacked or were ransacked and their priceless collections lost and scattered. Extant chronicles frequently mention tomes no longer available and quote works otherwise unknown. Rashīd al-Dīn detailed the extreme measures that he went to ensure that his own great chronicles would survive and yet despite such care and determination most of the original copies of his great work, painstakingly produced in all Iran's major urban centres, have disappeared. However, the recent discovery of not only Shirazi's little gem but of the substantial work of Majd al-Dīn Tabrizi, the *Safīna-ye Tabrīzī*, brings

Figure FM0.1 Dashi Namdakov's Chinggis Khan, Marble Arch, 2014

Chinggis Khan 'conquered' London in 2012 and his magnificent statue by the renowned artist Dashi Namdakov graced Marble Arch for a couple of years.

Source: Halcyon Gallery, New Bond St. © A. Bronnikov and Peter Mallett. Reproduced with permission.

hope for the future. Tabrizi's *Safīna* is a complete library of literary works including poetry, philosophy, history, theology, and scientific works, all meticulously copied out by a local man of means, Majd al-Dīn, in the 1320s. Tehran University has now reproduced a facsimile edition of the work which provides a unique insight into the intellectual milieu of the later Ilkhanate. However, more than this, the appearance of both these two works provides hope that in the future more such discoveries will be made and more of those very many missing tomes will eventually reappear for the edification of some very source-hungry scholars.

Acknowledgements

A number of people have helped me over the years as I slowly worked through this captivating and intriguing text. I was constantly emailing friends and colleagues, knocking on doors, dropping unexpectedly upon unsuspecting victims with a knowledge of Persian, anyone who could throw light on some of the obscure words, phrases, and usages which lay scattered throughout Shirazi's text. It was not an easy task and agreement was not always easy to find.

Especial thanks must go to Peter Jackson who never refused my requests for advice and guidance and who helped me unravel some of the more obscure passages. My colleague, Derek Mancini-Lander, has always opened his door to me whenever I came knocking and never failed to shine a light into the darkness. My thanks must also go to Florence Hodous who has always been willing to give up her time to check over my error-infected first drafts and correct the many inaccuracies of the early drafts.

I would like to thank Charlotte de Blois and Alison Ohta at the *Royal Asiatic Society* for permission to re-use some of the material from my own article on Shirazi's chronicle published in their Journal in October 2012.

And finally my thanks to my wife, Assumpta, and my two children, Oscar and Ella, who have put themselves through their A levels and university as I have been absorbed in Shirazi's thirteenth-century Iran.

I feel that Carole Hillenbrand and the Routledge team deserve a special mention since without their support this little historical gem would not have become available to the English-speaking world.

1 Introduction

The *Akhbār-i-Moghūlān dar Anbāneh-ye Quṭb* by Quṭb al-Dīn Maḥmūd ibn Mas^cūd Shīrāzī

The period between circa 1260 and the early 1300s has been described as a historiographical desert with the dearth of historical chronicles and absence of historical accounts having been caused by the Iranian Muslim world's apprehension at a prolonged period of infidel rule, a *fatrat*,[1] or interregnum, which ended with the production of the remarkable compendium of histories by the researchers of the *Rab'-Rashīdī*, Rashīd al-Dīn's academy in Tabriz.[2] Their collective hard work under the guidance of the polymath and exceptionally talented Rashīd al-Dīn produced the world's first universal history, the *Jāma^c al-tavārīkh*, to which the present work donated a sprinkling of information and words.

Juwaynī ended his own chronicle on the eve of the fall of Baghdad following the destruction of Alamut and the end to the 'blasphemous and heretical' regime of the Ismailis. Some saw ominous meaning in his silence on the 'events', the 'vāqi'a' of Baghdad, a silence that seemed to be broken only with the re-establishment of Muslim rule again in Iran.

However, Juwaynī was only partly silent and for good reason. First, his colleague, Naṡīr al-Dīn Ṫūsī (1201–74) provided a final chapter to Juwaynī's *History of the World Conqueror*, which covered the 'events' in Baghdad, while his own account finished more appropriately with the end of an era rather than the start of a new age. But perhaps more importantly, 'Aṫā Malik Juwaynī was no longer a court adviser with time on his hands to write and

1 See Judith Pfeiffer, "The Canonization of Cultural Memory", in Anna Akasoy et al. (eds.), *Rashīd al-Dīn: Agent and Mediator of Cultural Exchanges in Ilkhanid Iran* (London: The Warburg Institute, 2013), pp. 57–70.

2 An institution founded by Rashīd al-Dīn in Tabriz which comprised a scriptorium, libraries, lecture halls, mosques, and madresseh and which was twinned with the Hanlin academy in Khanbaliq (Beijing), contact facilitated through his friendship with the great Bolad Chingsang. See Thomas Allsen, *Culture and Conquest in Mongol Eurasia* (Cambridge: Cambridge University Press, 2001).

research at leisure but the governor of a large and important cosmopolis. Not only was his new position time consuming, but it was politically sensitive and his words and pronouncements were public property with his every syllable carrying political weight. As Baghdad's governor, his words were far more than likely to ruffle the feathers of someone, somewhere, about something than as Hulegu's PA whose thoughts and opinions would have had far more limited impact.

In fact, during this early period of Ilkhanid rule, local histories continued to be written, and Rashīd al-Dīn's collection of chronicles is just that, a collection of notes, observations, accounts, and records, which was being amassed in the decades prior to Ghazan's enthronement. The Ilkhans might have been infidels but they had been recognised as legitimate Iranian monarchs from the beginning as the great Sunni theologian, Bayḍawī, was keen to attest with his regularly updated historical pocket book, *Niżām al-tavārīkh*. The period between 1282 and 1295 was a period of unusually disruptive political activity in Ilkhanid Iran, a dynastic period (1258–1335) of general political stability, cultural prosperity, and certainly in the earlier decades, economic growth. The *Akhbār* only came to light a few years ago, not long after the discovery of the remarkable *Safīna-ye Tabrīz* dating from circa 1322–35 which certainly maintains the hope and possibility that other chronicles, short histories, and historical accounts might continue to come to light in the musty and neglected storerooms of Iranian academia.

The *Akhbār-i Moghūlān dar Anbāneh Quṭb* penned though not necessarily authored by Quṭb al-Dīn Shīrāzī (1236–1311),[3] outlines the early years of the Chinggisid empire, recounts the rule of Hulegu Khan and his son Abaqa, and finally, details the travails and ultimate demise and death of Abaqa's brother and would be successor, Ahmad Tegudar. It is an original and independent source and though it covers well-known events and personalities, it throws new light on these events and makes some startling and controversial claims concerning other matters that are only lightly touched upon elsewhere. Shīrāzī was a well-known, highly respected figure with access to key members of the ruling elite and to other centres of establishment power and influence including the ulema. He supplemented his scientific work with copy writing manuscripts which is why the authorship but not the penmanship of this work is in question.[4]

3 Sayyed ᶜAbd-Allāh Anwār, "Qoṭb-al-Din Širāzi", *Encyclopaedia Iranica*, Online edn, 2005, <www.iranicaonline.org/articles/qotb-al-din-sirazi#>. Accessed 10 February 2017.

4 Some parts of this introductory chapter originally appeared in an article about Shīrāzī's manuscript which appeared in the *Journal of the Royal Asiatic Society*. Those parts of the present chapter are appearing here with the kind permission of the editors of the *Journal of the Royal Asiatic Society*. George Lane, "Mongol News: The Akhbār-i *Moghūlān* dar

Quṭb al-Dīn Maḥmūd ibn Mas^c^ūd Shīrāzī

Quṭb al-Dīn Maḥmūd ibn Mas^c^ūd Shīrāzī (634–710/1236–1311) is best known for his association with Naṣīr al-Dīn Ṭūsī (d.1274) and his astrological and scientific work at the famous observatory of Maragha, in Iranian Azerbaijan. Born into a cultured and educated family, Quṭb al-Dīn received medical training from his father, Żiā' al-Dīn Mas^c^ud Kāzerunī, a well-connected physician and Sufi, who died when the boy was only 14, leaving his son's schooling in the hands of some of Shiraz's leading scholars. The young Quṭb al-Dīn delved into the complexities of Avicenna's *Qānun* along with Fakhr al-Dīn's commentaries and reputedly raised many issues with his tutors which he determined one day to answer in his own commentary. He succeeded his father at the Mozarfarī hospital in Shiraz as an ophthalmologist while still a teenager and continued his education under such luminaries of the *Qānun* as Kamāl al-Dīn Abu al-Khayr, Sharāf al-Dīn Zakī Bushkānī, and Shams al-Dīn Moḥammad Kishī until the age of about 24. He left the hospital to devote himself full time to scholarly pursuits when he heard about developments in the north of the country which offered an opportunity too great to ignore. Shīrāzī left Shiraz in 1260 and he is believed to have finally arrived at Ṭūsī's *Rasadkhāna* in 1262.

The Maragha complex of Ṭūsī's *Rasadkhāna* had gained in renown and stature as the Ilkhanate grew and benefitted from growing political stability, expanding trade links, and increasing cultural exchange. The complex comprised the famous observatory, Ṭūsī's library amassed from the intellectual riches of both Alamut and, much to the chagrin of the exiled Arabs in Cairo, of Baghdad's famed collections, a madressah and mosque, and the lecture halls and research laboratories of the *Rasadkhāna*. Ibn Fuwaṭī, Ṭūsī's chief librarian, who had been rescued from Baghdad, composed a mammoth biographical dictionary during his time in Maragha, based on information gleaned from the many scholars, researchers, and merchant travellers who availed themselves of this seat of learning which had fast been gaining an international as well as a regional reputation. Only the volumes of his biographical dictionary covering 'names' from ^c^*ayn* to *mīm* have survived and even these extant folios are a summary of the lost originals.[5] The Mamluk scholars in Cairo could only fume in resentful frustration as Maragha built

---

Anbāneh Qutb by Quṭb al-Dīn Maḥmūd ibn Mas^c^ūd Shīrāzī", *Journal of the Royal Asiatic Society*, Vol. 22, No. 3/4 (2012), pp. 541–559. doi:10.1017/S1356186312000375.

5 On Ibn Fuwaṭī's work at the *Rasadkhāna* library see Devlin DeWeese, "Cultural Transmission and Exchange in the Mongol Empire", in Linda Komaroff (ed.), *Beyond the Legacy of Genghis Khan* (Leiden and Boston: Brill, 2006), pp. 11–29.

Figure 1.1 Tusi's Observatory, The *Rasdakhana*, Maragha

Maragha was also the site of the scientist, Nasīr al-Dīn Ṭūsī's world famous observatory, the *Rasadkhan*, built for him by Hulegu, the first Ilkhan.

Photo by author

its reputation on the stolen waqf-supported, intellectual wealth of Baghdad that they considered rightfully theirs.

Their spokesman, the historian and man-of-letters, Ibn Aybak al-Ṣafadī (1296–1363) cursed Ṭūsī whom he accused of having persuaded Hulegu to award him Baghdad's libraries, 400,000 tomes, as acknowledgment for services rendered and advice given and expressed 'utter derision and humiliation' when he thought of the treachery of Ibn al-ᶜAlqamī who had been in secret correspondence with the approaching enemies of his master, the Caliph al-Mustaᶜṣim.[6] Certainly, the Persian scholars and clerics who flocked to Maragha felt no scruples or guilt in availing themselves of

6 See George Saliba, "Ilkhanid Patronage of Astronomers", in Linda Komaroff (ed.), *Beyond the Legacy of Genghis Khan* (Leiden and Boston: Brill, 2006), pp. 360–362; Ṣalāḥ al-Dīn Khalīl ibn Aybak al-Ṣafadī, *al-Wāfī bi al-Wafayāt*, vol. 1 (Wiesbaden: F. Steiner, 1981) on the fall of Baghdad, pp. 179–189, on Ṭūsī's role, 400,000 books in total from Baghdad, Syria and Jazira, pp. 184ff, cited in Saliba, p. 360.

Figure 1.2 Observatory foundations, Maragha

This is all that remains of Ṭūsī's Rasadkhana, the brick foundations preserved under a large plastic dome.

Photo by author

Ṭūsī's glittering prize and would not have agreed with al-Ṣafadī's assessment of Hulegu's honoured senior adviser Ṭūsī, as a thief and embezzler. Hulegu gave Ṭūsī authority over the distribution and control of waqfs, a highly controversial position, which allowed the wazir to lavish funds on his prestigious project, the *Rasadkhāna*, and freed Hulegu from having to find funding himself for such an expensive commitment. For Ṣafadī, Hulegu was in a win/win situation; he avoided financial responsibility for this monetary sponge while earning the loyalty of a key Iranian player for actualising his pet project.[7]

The complex was a magnet and other key political and cultural figures associated themselves with the *Rasadkhāna*. The existence of a collection of modified caves dug deep into the steep sides of the hill towering over the market town of Maragha is believed, though not proven, to be the remains of the Syriac church constructed on Hulegu's orders, for the bishop, Abu Faraj Mor Gregorios Bar Hebraeus. The cave entrances lie in the hillside below the site of the observatory which crowns the hilltop, giving the astronomers a panoramic view of the town, the mountain to the north, and the undulating land levelling off towards Lake Urmia in the west. Bar Hebraeus wrote his own great chronology in Maragha and in the introduction to this great historical work he expresses his gratitude and indebtedness to Ṭūsī and his library.

From its inauguration, the observatory attracted scholars from all over Iran and beyond. Shīrāzī resumed his education under Ṭūsī, adding astronomy to medicine, ophthalmology, the *Qānun*, and the other sciences in which he had already been schooled. Theology had of course comprised a major element of his early education and he had received his *Kherqā*, a Sufi robe, from Najīb-al-Dīn Ali b. Bozḡosh Shīrāzī. His father had received his own *Kherqā* from the renowned Shehāb-al-Dīn ᶜUmar Sohravardī. Shīrāzī had been a precocious and avid student of theology, but he was a true polymath and he matched Ṭūsī's passion for the stars, becoming instrumental in the composition of the astronomical tables (*Zij*) for which the Maragha observatory became justly celebrated.

A revealing anecdote which has survived from the comparatively short time that Shīrāzī stayed in Maragha, recounts how the Ilkhan, Hulegu, piqued with his trusted adviser, Ṭūsī, revealed to the young scholar that there was only one reason that he did not have Ṭūsī executed. The Ilkhan confided in Shīrāzī that he needed Ṭūsī to finish the *Zij* to which revelation the earnest Quṭb al-Dīn responded by assuring Hulegu that he should not fear because he would be quite capable of finishing the tables for him

7 Saliba, p. 361.

Figure 1.3 Bar Hebraeus' Church, beneath Tusi's Observatory

Hulegu also built the Syriac bishop, Bar Hebreus, a church of which these caves situated beneath observatory could well have been an integral part.

Photo by author

without Ṭūsī's assistance. Later, the bemused Ṭūsī asked his star pupil if this story were true, and the guileless Quṭb assured him that it was. Warned that Hulegu was unlikely to have appreciated Shīrāzī's ironic banter, Quṭb assured his master that he had not been joking but had been quite serious.[8] It is worth noting that in Ṭūsī's later records of the *Rasadkhāna*, Shīrāzī's name is absent from the list of his assistants despite the great deal of important work that he had devoted to the composition of the tables. Rashīd al-Dīn and Waṣṣāf similarly omit mention of Quṭb al-Dīn in their accounts of the Maragha observatory. No mention of the observatory or library is made in

8 Ghiyath al-Dīn Khwandmīr, *Tārīkh-i-Ḥabib al-Siyar*, vol. 3 (Tehran: Ketābkhāneh Khayam, 1954/1333), pp. 116–117; Wheeler Thackston (tr.), *Classical Writings of the Mediaeval Islamic World: Persian Histories of the Mongol Dynasties*, "Habibu's-Siyar: The Reign of the Mongol and the Turk Genghis Khan" by Khwandamir, tome 3 (London and New York: I.B. Tauris, 2012), p. 65.

"Shīrāzī's"[9] chronicle though this is hardly the only important omission. However, confirmation of Shīrāzī's crucial contribution to the *Zij* is attested to indirectly when in his will, the *waṣiya*, Ṭūsī advises his son, Aṣil-al-Din, to work with Shīrāzī on the completion of the astronomical tables. The significance of these omissions is a matter for conjecture.

As well as erudite and voluminous commentaries and analyses of Ṭūsī's astronomical and occasional astrological calculations, Shīrāzī produced his own novel mathematical solutions to the problems with which this learned elite at the *Rasadkhāna* were grappling along with his own ideas on, among other things, the motion of the planets and other heavenly bodies. However, his comparatively short stay in Maragha ended after he travelled to Khorasan with Ṭūsī and then decided against returning and instead remained in Jovein to study under Najm-al-Dīn Kātebī Qazvīnī.[10]

Sometime after 1268, it is recorded that Shīrāzī travelled widely around the country ending up in Anatolia where it is known that he encountered the Sufi poet, Jalāl al-Dīn Rūmī.[11] While in Konya he again resumed his studies, with Ṣadr-al-Dīn Qunawī (d. 1274) guiding his progress. When the governor of Rum, the Parvana Moᶜīn-al-Dīn Solaymān, appointed Qunawī as the qadi of Sivas and Malatya, Shīrāzī accompanied him to his new post, all the time increasing his circle of friends and contacts. It was Quṭb al-Dīn who was chosen by the Ilkhan, Ahmad Tegudar, to travel to Egypt in 1282 as his representative to the court of Sayf-al-Dīn Qalāwun (r. 1279–90) to whom he was introduced as the Ilkhan's chief judge. It was on his return from Egypt that he began work on the *Akhbār-i-Moghūlān* but strangely no mention of such an embassy appears in the chronicle.[12] After settling in Syria where he taught two of the works of Avicenna, the Qānun on medicine, and the Shefāᶜ on philosophy, Quṭb al-Dīn moved to Tabriz and it was there that he died at the age of 75 and was buried in the Charandāb Cemetery, close to the tomb of Qadi Bayḍāwī.[13]

Quṭb al-Dīn Shīrāzī is remembered as an intellectual giant in an age of exceptional scholars. However, he is famous not only for his prolific

9 Because of the questions over the authorship of this chronicle, 'Shīrāzī' refers to the author of the *Akhbār-ye-Moghūlān* whereas Shīrāzī refers to the historical figure of Quṭb al-Dīn.

10 Ḥāfeẓ Ḥosayn ibn al-Kerbelā'ī, *Rauẓāt al-Jenān va Jennāt al-Jenān*, vol. 1 (Tehran: BTNK, 1965/1344), p. 324.

11 Kerbelā'ī, vol. 1, pp. 326–327.

12 It is probable that a number of pages from the original manuscript have been lost since there are many lacunae in the extant copy.

13 Qāshānī, ᶜAbd al-Qasem, *Tārīkh-i-Ūljaytū*, ed. Mahin Hambley (Tehran: BTNK, 1969/1348), pp. 118–119; Ḥāfeẓ Ḥosayn, I, pp. 324, 331; Faṣiḥ Khwāfi, *Mujmal-i-Faśīḥī*, ed. Maḥmūd Farrukhī, vol. 3 (Tus, Mashhad: Ketabferushi Bastan, 1962/1341), p. 18; on Bayḍāwī see Melville "From Adam to Abaqa . . . ", n.69.

intellectual output and the passion with which he acquired knowledge, but for his good-nature and humour, a zest for life, and a generosity of spirit. Khwandamīr records that "his major characteristic was mirth, and he constantly told jokes and pleasantries."[14] He was known as a proficient chess player and a musician who entertained with the *rubāb* and he cultivated a wide circle of diverse friends and acquaintances. Hitherto he had not been noted as an historian, but his many contacts in the political world and his influence with the 'movers and shakers' of the Ilkhanate made him an ideal commentator and observer. However, Quṭb al-Dīn has now been credited with the transcription rather than the authorship of this newly edited, short history of the early Ilkhanate though the extent of his input and the degree to which the content reflects his views is certainly debatable.

The Akhbār-ye-Moghūlān

The actual date of writing is given early in this annotated chronology as 680/1280, where, on the first page of the manuscript (folio 22b) listing the rulers of the house of Jochi and their dominion over the Qipchaq steppe[15] (*Khifjaq* in text), it states that "after him [Monkū Timūr], Tūtā Monkū who is pādeshāh at this time (*sā'at*), that is the year 680."[16]

Known more for his thoughts on astronomy and theology, Quṭb al-Dīn's work as a calligrapher is often overlooked. In fact, a considerable number of mediaeval Persian manuscripts from collections around the world are written in the hand of Shīrāzī including the codex from which the present historical chronicle is taken. This codex is currently in the library of the Ayatollah al-ᶜUẓmā Mar'ashī Najafī in Qom (MS Marᶜashī 12868) and it remains accessible for researchers. For many years the codex had been broken up and dispersed before being collected, collated and rebound, and eventually acquired by the current library in Qom. A detailed study of the Marᶜashī codex by Reza Pourjavady and Sabine Schmidtke appeared in 2007 in *Studia Iranica*. As well as a careful itemised analysis of the contents of the codex, Schmidtke and Pourjavady revealed the extent of Shīrāzī's work as a copyist, demonstrating that he penned not only many of his own works but those of his contemporaries, including his colleague Nasir al-Dīn Ṭūsī.

The Shīrāzī codex, containing this short history of the early Ilkhanate, comprises 147 leaves and originally belonged to the library of Rashīd al-Dīn

14 Khwandmīr, p. 116; tr. Thackston, p. 65.

15 The Qipchaq Turks, also known as Cumans, Polovtsy, or Pechenegs inhabited the western Eurasian steppe from Kazakhstan to the west. Under Batu they became known as the Great Horde, the Golden Horde, or the Qipchaq Khanate.

16 Shīrāzī, p. 20.

in the *Rab^c-e Rasīdī*, Tabriz, as indicated by stamps on some of the leaves bearing the insignia '*waqf-e-ketābkhāna Rashīdī'*. The folios are incomplete and there are leaves missing from many sections including from the beginning and the end of the codex itself. The codex has undergone various preservation measures and now contains 14 sections whose disparate contents throw much light on the intellectual interests of Quṭb al-Dīn Shīrāzī and the cultural milieu in which he lived. There are various Persian and Arabic quatrains and poems including verse by ᶜUmar Khayyam, fragments of works on philosophy, extracts from the sayings of Plato, extensive fragments from the work of Tāj al-Dīn Shahrestānī, various quotations from pre-Islamic Persian and Greek thinkers, large tracts by his contemporary, the Jewish philosopher Ibn Kammūna ,and Samaw'al al-Maghribī's '*Silencing the Jews*' (*Ifḥām al-Yahūd*), and also, of course, the Ilkhanid chronicle penned if not composed by Quṭb al-Dīn.

The chronicle was composed between 1281 and 1285 but gives no indication as to its authorship or whether it was a collaborative project though the repetition of certain phrases and verb forms throughout the work suggests one author. No irrefutable evidence exists to prove the argument either way. Īraj Afshār, the editor of the Persian text, suggests that there are various external reasons for presuming that Quṭb al-Dīn is the actual author, but at the same time he cites two reasons for doubting Shīrāzī's authorship. Firstly, there is the inconsistency in the spelling of certain names found throughout the chronicle. This however was not an uncommon phenomenon at this time and since no system of efficient proof reading existed it is hardly surprising that errors occurred. Afshār points out that variations in spelling within a single document were common at this time. Secondly, there is the claim by the author of this chronicle that he had been at Hulegu's court 'very often' [*bisiyār uqāt*][17] whereas, the editor recalls, there is only one recorded meeting between Shīrāzī and Hulegu Khan when in 660AH Ṭūsī took his colleague to the Ilkhanid court. Despite these many visits of the author of the chronicle to Hulegu's court, there remains only this one cited reference to Shīrāzī meeting Hulegu, a discrepancy which at best constitutes flimsy evidence either way.[18]

The present pagination of the folios no longer corresponds to the original order of writing. Īraj Afshār is responsible for re-ordering the folios and arranging them in the correct chronological sequence as he explains in his introduction to the *Akhbār-i Mughulān*. Both the original and the chronological order of the folios are given in his introduction along with a summary

17 Shīrāzī, p. 22.
18 Shīrāzī, pp. 9–10.

of each section and sheet. However, whether by loss or through design, the chronology of these early decades of Ilkhanid rule do not flow smoothly and lacunae of differing lengths occur intermittently. The four years between 658 and 662, and the eight years between 667 and 675 are missing. Other gaps then appear throughout the remainder of the history. The seven-year gap between the years 667 through to 675 is the longest omission and the final year, 683, receives the fullest and most detailed treatment. As well as the problem with the erroneous rebinding of the original folios, the editor has also had his own problems with his edited version. The page for the year 656 has inexplicably appeared on page 41 whereas it should appear as page 35.

The appearance of this previously little-known volume of chronological notes and anecdotes dating from the second half of the thirteenth century, detailing among other events the fall of Alamut, the siege of Baghdad, and the collapse of relations between Ahmad Tegudar and his nephew, Arghun Khan, is both welcome and very exciting. Published in the holy city of Qum, Iran, this slender tome contains a short introduction with a skeletal outline of the chronology and the corresponding events, an edited text, and also a facsimile copy of the original manuscript. Why someone of Quṭb al-Dīn Shirāzī's stature should task himself with such a work and why he has not been awarded any acknowledgement for his efforts remains a mystery, but his contributions to our knowledge of this turbulent and controversial period of Iranian history are undoubtedly valuable and offer insights on major events and characters, some details of which are not found elsewhere despite the possible use of this manuscript as a source for Rashīd al-Dīn's *Jāmaʿ al-Tavārīkh* or the use of a common source by both histories. The extent of Shīrāzī's involvement in the authorship of the manuscript remains uncertain and this controversy is explored in Afshār's introductory pages, but it must be presumed that Shīrāzī harboured sympathy for the views expressed in this record and the greatest respect for the author or even authors of the chronicle.

Īraj Afshār presents the text with a minimal amount of commentary and there is also very little scholarly analysis which invites therefore future study and research on this important text. The language of the chronology is plain, direct, and stripped of the usual Persian excesses and hyperbole so characteristic of the style of that time though various idiosyncrasies do occur for example, to specify just one, the use of '*na-māndan*' to signify death and '*birūn na-mānad*' meaning 'not to remain outside' that is 'to die'.

Birth of an empire

The short introductory chapter, entitled "The beginning of the Mongol government and the advent of Chinggis Khan", opens with the names of the Great Khan's forefathers and the date of Chinggis Khan's emergence which is given in five calendars: the Arab calendar at AH599, the Rūmiyān calendar 1514 [sic], the Zoroastrian calendar of Yazdegerd III 572, and both the Uyghur calendar and the Chinese calendar recording the year of the Pig,[19] corresponding to 1202/3 CE. However, it is not clear to exactly what events the dates refer, 1202/3 being a year prior to Temujin's enthronement, unless they refer to the Baljuna episode which is considered the turning point in Chinggis Khan's career when he 'hit rock bottom' and began the fight back.[20] This generous serving of dates which reflects the cosmopolitanism and global awareness and attitude in the author, is mirrored in certain other textual sources from this era, and it contrasts with the more usual parochial outlook commonly found at this time in the local sources whether Arab, Persian, or Armenian. However, other examples of this use of multiple calendars, like the early fourteenth-century Persian tombstone unearthed in Hangzhou which belonged to an amir and merchant resident in the former Song capital, along with a mid-fifteenth-century mosque stele from the same provenance, while no doubt reflecting the same sophisticated and worldly nature, can be more readily explained by their location far from home on the other side of the planet. They belonged to an expatriate, international community.[21] The use of these multiple calendars at home in Iran suggests either that the small community residing at the *Rasadkhāna* of Maragha was itself international or that it was composed of members of the Toluid elite, men who travelled from west to east and back again and who regarded themselves as citizens of a dynamic and growing empire where the traditional limitations and labels of identity no longer applied, and the old restrictions of religion, class, and family could no longer constrain.[22]

With the dates establishing the author's attitude and world view rather than a historically precise moment in time, the tone of the chronicle is set. Chinggis Khan is introduced with an anecdote from the 'lean years' when at Baljuna his core supporters pledged their loyalty and fidelity. The story or rather the topos relates how Chinggis Khan along with 70 of his faithful followers were stranded in the desert at Wadi Baljuna[23] without food. One

19 Shīrāzī, p. 19.

20 See Francis Woodman Cleaves, "The Historicity of the Baljuna Covenant", *Harvard Journal of Asiatic Studies*, Vol. 18, No. 3/4 (Dec., 1955), pp. 357–421.

21 See George Lane, *The Phoenix Mosque* (London: Gingko Library, 2018).

22 See George Lane, "The Phoenix Mosque of Hangzhou 杭州凤凰寺" and A.H. Morton, "Muslim Gravestones in the Phoenix Mosque in Hangzhou 杭州凤凰寺的穆斯林墓碑", *Qinghua Yuanshi* 清華元氏, No. 1, edn 1 (2011).

23 It is uncertain if Baljuna refers to a lake or a river, but the presence of mud means water. Its location in Inner Asia is also disputed by this and other matters concerning Baljuna are discussed in Igor de Rachewiltz, *The Secret History of the Mongols* (Leiden and Boston: Brill, 2006), §182, §183, pp. 655–664.

Figure 1.4 Hulegu's Mother's Tomb, Maragha

"Maragha became Hulegu's capital in Iran. Though she never actually visited Iran, this tomb-tower celebrates his mother, Sorqaqtani Beki, who was also the mother of two great khans, Qubilai and Mongke."

Photo by author

of his soldiers manages to shoot down a desert sparrow and the bird is then roasted and offered to the Khan. The Khan orders that the bird be divided into 70 parts from which he then took his share, no larger than any one of the other portions. As a result of such righteousness and exemplary behaviour, the text continues, all the people became devotees and followers of Chinggis Khan and gave their souls to his cause.

The pledges of loyalty and faith offered at Baljuna, circa 1203, mark the turning point in the fortunes of Temujin, the future Chinggis Khan. All those who kept the faith and remained committed to their Khan, the Baljunatu who "drank the muddied waters of the lake",[24] were eventually awarded for their faith and fidelity. This was the lowest point in Temujin's career after which his rise was relentless until in 1206 he was finally recognised as the Great Khan of the Peoples of the Nine Tongues and the Peoples of the Felt-walled Tents, and he was proclaimed Chinggis Khan, mighty, hard khan, unifier of the Turco-Mongol tribes.

By 1206 Temujin had exacted revenge on those who had inflicted pain on him and his family and he moved to consolidate absolute power into his hands and eradicate any other source of authority that could challenge his ambitions. He killed his *anda* (blood-brother)[25] Jamuqa, whose prestige had held the potential to split the nomadic people of the Eurasian steppe and he removed the manipulative Teb-Tengri, the charismatic shaman, whose endorsement had assured Chinggis the throne. Teb-Tengri was ambitious and hungry for some of the authority that he had allowed Chinggis Khan but when he moved to curb the Khan's power, he sealed his own fate and in traditional Mongol fashion, he was seized and his spine was cracked.

The Great Khan's problem was to maintain the unity and impetus of those first euphoric days for he realised that loyalty was only maintained with the bread of victory and the wine of plunder, so he first dissolved the tribes and recreated them as a single decimalised body under the command of those who had pledged loyalty at Baljuna and who now became his commanders of a Tuman (10,000). Promotion was the reward of loyalty and ability in the multi-ethnic army where tribal identity had been subsumed to a meritocracy. In the past, tribe was pitted against tribe and wealth was always at the expense of the weak. One tribe grew fat while another became lean and the steppe fed of itself. Now the Chinggisids faced the world as one and as one from the steppe, the Chinggisids moved out into the sown, the sedentary, and urbanised world, and their first real target was China.

24 See de Rachewiltz, 2006, §182, §183, pp. 655–658; John Andrew Boyle Juwaynī, *Genghis Khan: History of the World Conqueror*, tr. intro. David Morgan (Manchester: Manchester University Press, 1997), pp. 37, 87; ᶜAṭāᶜ Malik Juwaynī, *Tārīkh-i-Jahān Gushā*, ed. Mohamad Qazvīnī, vol. 3 (Leyden and London: Brill and Luzac, 1937), pp. 27, 67–68; Francis Woodman Cleaves, "The Historicity of the Baljuna Convenant", *Harvard Journal of Asiatic Studies*, Vol. 18, No. 3/4 (Dec., 1955), pp. 357–421.

25 Close friendships were sealed with a blood pact when blood from two small wounds was mingled. Anda were considered closer than family.

The Toluids

So, with the euphoria of Wadi Baljuna starts Quṭb al-Dīn's history of the Mongols and the Ilkhans up until the ascension of Arghun Khan on Friday, 27th Jumāda I, 683 (11th August 1285), and it is clear the regard in which the author holds Chinggis Khan, the grandfather of the regime under which he served. The regime, the Ilkhanate, under which Shīrāzī served, had been founded in 1258 by Hulegu Khan, the younger brother of the new Great Khan (Qa'an), Mongke. Mongke, the oldest of four sons of Tolui Khan (d.1232), the youngest son of Chinggis, came to power circa 1250 in a coup d'état following the death of his cousin, Guyuk (d.1248). The Toluids, as they became known, had been nurtured, educated, and groomed for power by their remarkable mother, Sorqaqtani Beki (d.1250). Mongke, in order to consolidate his power base, had sent his brother Qubilai to the east to maintain his grip and continue his conquest of China, while he dispatched his brother, Hulegu, to the west where he was welcomed by the peoples of Iran who joined Hulegu's forces in the conquest of Baghdad and the Arab lands and in the destruction of the 'heretical' Ismailis. Toluid rule was marked by compromise and a united administration. The Toluids formed a multi-ethnic state and administration. The Ilkhanate (1235–1335) and the Yuan dynasty (1269–1370) were multicultural and integrated and stood in contrast to the rest of the Mongol empire from which they split following Mongke's death in 1259.

The author's, and by implication "Shirāzī's", sympathetic view of the Chinggisids is made clear from the start. This was a regime of which he felt himself a part and an empire of which he saw himself both a player and a beneficiary. He summarises the Chinggisid conquests and the individual rulers before observing that now with the ascension of Mongke Qa'an "The wolf and the sheep drank water together",[26] a sentiment expressed also by the contemporary poet, Saᶜdī, in the introduction to his anecdotal poem, *Gulistan*.[27] Saᶜdī, also from Shiraz, had returned to Iran after many years wandering, probably in the Arab world, where he had sought an escape from the chaos which reigned in his native land, Iran. The anarchy which had prevailed after the collapse, in 1222, of the Khwarazmshah's cruel reign had lasted three decades until the advent of Hulegu and his imposition of order on the troubled lands of Iran. The poet returned to Shiraz with the country now under the control of "tigers who had abandoned

26 Shīrāzī, p. 20.

27 Sa'di of Shiraz, *The Gulistan* or *Rose Garden*, tr. Francis Gladwin, intro. and ed. Kamal Haj Sayyed Javadi (Tehran: al-Hoda, 2000/1379), p. 14.

the nature of tigers"[28] and he eventually made personal contacts with the ruling regime.[29]

Echoing Juwaynī, who was also particularly effusive in his praise for the new Qa'an, Mongke, the author, hereafter "Shirāzī", portrays the Toluid ascendancy in very positive terms, typified in such statements as "The like of the days of justice and equity that dominated during his (Mongke's) days are few"[30] but adds that after taking measures "such as killing, beating, shackling and the like, not one person from among those that had been co-conspirators in opposition remained alive but not one innocent person suffered loss."[31] Mongke's coup is depicted more as a return to just rule after a period of misdirection, in keeping with the advice of the 'kingmaker' Batu Khan, ruler of the Qipchaq Khanate, the Golden Horde, whose endorsement legitimised Mongke's sovereignty. "Shirāzī's" final observation claims that

> When the work of those provinces, Turkestan, and Khitai, and Oxiana, and Tibet, and Tangut, and many other provinces were put in order [*rāst kard*], he sent his own brother Hulegu in the direction of [the river] Jayhūn that is to say the provinces of the Arabs and the Persians ['Arab va 'Ajam] in order to put them in order [*rāst konad*].[32]

Batu Khan and the Jochids

During the harsh days of Chinggis Khan's early life, his decisive actions were to have long-lasting repercussions. Following his wedding to his childhood sweetheart, Borte, the newlyweds were waylaid and out-numbered by a marauding band of Merkit tribesmen intent on murder, plunder, and replenishing the tribes stock of females in the traditional steppe practice of kidnapping and bride-snatching. In fact, Chinggis Khan's mother, Hoelun, had herself been seized from the Merkits by Yesugei, his murdered father, for which this current act might well have been revenge. Temujin had decided moments before the raiders attacked that he would flee and leave his bride and her mother to their fate, reckoning that if he stayed he would certainly be killed and by his death he would be sentencing those two women to a lifetime's servitude and mistreatment. Within months, Temujin had ensured military support and was soon in a position to launch a counter-attack on the

28 Sa'dī, p. 61.
29 A.J. Arberry, *Shiraz: Persian City of Saints and Poets* (Norman: University of Oklahoma Press, 1960), pp. 133–135.
30 Shīrāzī, p. 20.
31 Shīrāzī, p. 20.
32 Shīrāzī, p. 21.

Merkit camp to re-claim his women. However, Borte returned to his camp and was soon found to be pregnant and Chinggis Khan's first-born carried the stigma of a questionable paternity not only for the rest of his life but for the life of his descendants. For Chinggis the matter was closed and Jochi was his first-born, his son and his heir, but for others the matter was never closed and the *Secret History* records the taunts that Jochi was forced to endure. Chaghadai in particular, railed against Jochi becoming his father's successor as Great Khan. "How can we let ourselves be ruled by this bastard offspring of the Merkit?"[33] In fact, Jochi died before his father and so an explosive situation was avoided but thereafter, the Jochids, who had been granted the lands in the west "where Tatar hoof has trod"[34] under Prince Batu (d.1255) were content to remain autonomous king-makers rather than aspiring to the Qa'anate throne themselves. The European missionary, William of Rubruck, assumed that Batu enjoyed equal status to the Great Khan Mongke when he was received by Batu as he travelled through the Qipchaq Khanate on his way to the royal court in Qaraqorum.[35]

Chinggis Khan had awarded the Jochids the lands to the west but the boundaries were ambiguously defined. Certainly, during the years 1222 to 1256 when Iran was under ineffective martial law and often at the mercy of Ismaili bands, as well as Khwarazmian brigands, and other armed elements, the Jochids maintained nominal control through military commanders generally answerable to Batu. Batu's attitude to Hulegu's assumption of power was never made clear since he died before Hulegu had become established, but once relations between the Jochids and the Toluids had deteriorated the demarcation line "where Tatar hoof had trod" became a source of bitter dispute. Though "Shīrāzī" does not refer to this episode, he observes the deterioration of the relationship between the two parties.

Hulegu's journey west[36]

The *Akhbār-ye-Moghūlān* does not dwell on Hulegu's journey as does Juwaynī's chronicle. Juwaynī was an eye witness in his capacity as personal adviser to Hulegu and he would have had to meet and make arrangements for all the many dignitaries, rulers, ambassadors, envoys, and well-wishers

33 Igor de Rachewiltz, §254, pp. 922–937.

34 Juwaynī, Boyle, p. 42; Qazvīnī, p. 31.

35 William of Rubruck, *The Mission of Friar William of Rubruck: His Journey to the Court of the Great Khan Möngke 1253–1255*, tr. Peter Jackson, ed. David Morgan (London: Hakluyt, 1990), pp. 19, 180, ch. 23.

36 For a detailed account of Hulegu's journey, see John Masson Smith jnr in Komaroff, 2006, pp. 111–134.

who came to greet this 'World Conqueror'. Instead, in the *Akhbār*, the vast extent of the conquests is repeatedly emphasised, though some geographical references seem rather questionable, and the ambitions for total conquest that were still harboured as Hulegu moved westward are underlined with the explicit threats made to the still unconquered Arabs also recorded. But coupled with the threats of violence are reminders of the justice which '*īl*' [obedience, loyalty, and submission] can bring and the fact that word of these conquests and the justice of the Mongol edicts had even reached the lands of the Franks and the Rūmiyān.[37]

Hulegu's first appointment after crossing the Jayhūn (Oxus) was with the despised *mulāhadeh*,[38] the Ismailis, though the language used in reference to these 'feared heretics' has none of the loathing and almost pathological hatred evident in the writing of Juwaynī and other Sunni commentators. Though the line between Sunni and Shi'ite was not so clearly defined as today, ill-feeling between the communities was often strong. It is likely that the Sunni establishment grossly exaggerated the military threat posed by the Ismailis. The Fatimid state was long gone and the Nizari Ismailis[39] possessed no standing army and at most could launch raids against merchant caravans or isolated villages. The Sunni establishment feared the influence and political machinations of the Nizaris. They feared that they would strike a deal with the Chinggisids and that they would replace them as the spokesmen of Islam and advisers to the Great Khan, hence their embassy to Mongke's coronation and their warnings of the Ismaili threat to Iran and also to the Royal court at Qaraqorum itself. Alamut and other Nizari castles already attracted scholars and thinkers to their libraries and halls where free debate was encouraged. The Ismailis had always been great patrons of education and learning and, of course, they still are, just as they have always practised charity and there is evidence that they peddled their influence along with their charity in mediaeval Iran.[40] Though it is clear that the Sunni establishment despised the Nizaris, that contempt was not shared by the Shi'ites and "Shīrāzī" remains mainly neutral in his description of the Nizaris and the conquest of their strongholds. For example, the claim that the young Rukn al-Dīn, the Khwarshāh, murdered his father a short time before Hulegu's arrival is not repeated in his account.

37 Shīrāzī, p. 22.

38 'heretic', a term commonly applied to the Ismailis.

39 For a concise explanation for the various Ismaili manifestations see Bernard Lewis, *The Assassins: A Radical Sect in Islam* (London: Weidenfeld and Nicolson, 1967).

40 See Rashīd al-Dīn, 1994, p. 985; Thackston's translation in the 2012 I.B. Taurus edn. has clear references to the pagination of the 1994 Persian edn. of Rawshan & Mūsawī.

The writer goes into great detail in describing the preparation that had gone into the planning of Hulegu's advance. After a summary of the many countries that had submitted to Hulegu's forces and an account of the justice that had been delivered as these lands were 'liberated' [*mastakhlas*], witnessed by the author on his many trips to Hulegu's court, a detailed description of the armaments that Hulegu had brought with him to deal with the perceived threat from the *mulāhadeh* is given. The precise picture that emerges of the giant crossbow deployed against the Ismaili castles recalls Juwaynī's *Kamān-i-Gav* and the illustration from the *Wu Jing Zong Yao* (武經總要)[41] of 1044 of a lethal machine quite capable of delivering explosive devices. These powerful crossbows were capable of delivering heavily re-enforced arrows wrapped in leather with deadly precision over great distances, to hit moving targets, a 'vulture [or] eagle in flight high in the mountains' or strapped together to pound a castle's walls and ramparts. Whether the Chinggisid forces were employing explosives at this stage, a view strongly supported by the Yuan scholar, Stephen Haw,[42] and whether the word 'batān' or possibly 'panbeh' refers to some kind of explosive material is an intriguing possibility. To sustain the slow moving army that accompanied these massive machines, provisions had already been put in place by Arghun Aqa and other advance commanders, as reported by Juwayni in his history of these events, "emirs and local rulers . . . began to prepare provisions (*'ulūfa*) and get together *tuzghu* or offerings of food; and they set down their offerings at every stage (of the army's advance)."[43] "Shīrāzī" itemises some of the preparation that was in place to meet the demands of this vast body of men that was launched onto the Iranian plateau.

> And from all the provinces they brought out provisions and supplies without limit and beyond compare. They set off by donkey, camel and cow and asses and such like. They had brought limitless noodles and cooked porridge (*Tatum ash, Tatumaj*),[44] and pounded millet (*gāvrus-i kufteh*) from the provinces of Khitai and Uyghuristan to the foot of Alamut and Mimundaz and that castle, and every half farhang they

41 "*Collection of the Most Important Military Techniques*" was a Chinese military compendium written in 1044 AD, by Zeng Gongliang (曾公亮), Ding Du (丁度), and Yang Weide (楊惟德).

42 See Stephen Haw, "Gunpowder and the Mongols", *JRAS*, forthcoming.

43 ᶜAtāᶜ Malik Juwaynī, *Tārīkh-i-Jahān Gushā*, ed. Mohamad Qazvīnī, vol. 3 (London: Leyden and Brill, Luzac, 1937), p. 94; tr. John Andrew Boyle, intro. David Morgan, *Genghis Khan: History of the World Conqueror* (Manchester: Manchester University Press, 1997), p. 609.

44 See Paul Buell and Eugene Anderson, *Soup for the Qan* (London and New York: Kegan Paul International, 2010), p. 298.

had stacked ample flour and rice and necessities /ingredients (staples) in bags of fine linen so that everywhere were found great hills [of provisions].[45]

The huge war machine that is so precisely described had been transported from Turkestan along with trained experts. Upon its arrival on the borders of Khorasan, written orders and messengers were dispatched to the *malūk* and *pādeshāhān*[46] of the provinces. In these messages, Hulegu Khan solemnly pledged that if the royal recipients of his messages should undertake to assist him with troops, armaments, and military supplies in his forthcoming confrontation with the *mulāhadeh*, he would be under an obligation to provide peace and security for them and their provinces. Should they decline his invitation Hulegu would deal with them after he was free from the Ismaili business and he emphasised that later, any excuses that they might offer him would not be accepted. The menace lurking in his message was almost palpable and the author of this history itemises the response to Hulegu's request. The Atabeg of Shiraz, the sultans of Rum, the kings of Khorasan, Sistan, Mazanderan, Kirman, Rustamdar, Shirwan, Gorjestan, Iraq, Azerbayjan, Arran, and Luristan and some other provincial representatives all duly arrived. Others sent their brothers or relatives and they all sent men, military supplies, provisions, and gifts and placed themselves at Hulegu Khan's service.[47]

The writer's point is clear. Hulegu Khan operated with the support of the rulers of the whole country. The account of Hulegu's slow negotiations with Alamut, culminating in the young Rukn al-Dīn's final surrender, do not differ from other accounts in any significant ways though there is the suggestion that pestilence (*wabā*)[48] proved a factor in the reluctant surrender of the Ismaili castle of Lamasar.[49] The scale of the military operation is stressed from the start, with the claim that the siege of the first castle, GirdKuh, was "such as nobody had ever seen [before]".[50] The castle set a formidable task for the assailants. A moat had been dug around the fortified outer walls that protected the houses which lay between the outer walls and another inner wall and moat. This whole complex of walls and moats surrounded and protected

45 Shīrāzī, p. 24.
46 pl. malik, pādeshāh – ruler, king.
47 Shīrāzī, pp. 22–23.
48 See Lawrence I. Conrad, "Ta'un and Waba': Conceptions of Plague and Pestilence in Early Islam", *Journal of the Economic and Social History of the Orient*, Vol. 25, No. 3 (1982), pp. 268–307.
49 Shīrāzī, p. 28.
50 Shīrāzī, p. 25.

the innermost buildings to which access was further restricted by more moats and ramparts. After 'a day or two' with the operation proving more difficult than anticipated, Hulegu ordered his top commanders to initiate a prolonged siege which resulted 'after a year more or less' in the deaths of a great many of the besieged from pestilence. News was brought to the Ismaili leader, the Khwarshāh, ᶜAlā al-Dīn to inform him that not a man remained alive in Gird-Kuh and that the castle was lost. His response was to order the mobilisation of a hundred men under the command of Moqdam al-Dīn Moḥammad Mobāraz who was able to lead his troop through enemy lines and into the castle itself, suffering only one casualty, a man who fell into the moat and broke his leg. Though this story appears in Rashīd al-Dīn, the later version carries important embellishments, for example that Mobāraz and his men each carried two maunds [app. 37 kgs] of henna and three maunds of salt for the sick of GirdKuh in the belief that henna was a cure for pestilence. Other slight differences and additions suggest that Rashīd al-Dīn had additional sources of information.[51] Once in the castle Mobāraz and his men were able to strengthen the defences and continued to defy the enemy outside for another 20 years. "Shīrāzī" adds that finally after 20 years the defiant Ismailis surrendered and came down from their fortress only to be seized and summarily executed.[52]

The text does not dwell on the suspicious murder in 653 of ᶜAlā al-Dīn Moḥammad, the semi-divine Ismaili leader and the assumption of power by his young son, Rukn al-Dīn, known as the Khwarshāh. The short opening paragraph for this year, 653, simply states that a trusted and close servant of ᶜAlā' al-Dīn Moḥammad killed him, describing the man as a '*shakhsī-ye mortad*', an apostate, the standard derogatory term for an Ismaili.[53] Rashīd al-Dīn repeats the widely held belief that the Khwarshāh was indirectly responsible for his father's death and Juwaynī provides the detail and background to the complex father-son relationship.[54] "Shīrāzī's" account is shorter than both Rashīd al-Dīn's and Juwaynī's, but the inclusion of slight differences suggests that it might have had an independent source. "Shīrāzī" relates that Hulegu thundered down unexpectedly fast to surround the area where the Khwarshāh was camped, but that his arrival was hampered by extremely heavy rain.

51 Rashīd al-Dīn, *Jāmi' al-Tavārīkh*, ed. Moḥammad Rawshan and Mustafa Musavī (Tehran: Nashr Elborz, 1994/1373), p. 982.

52 Shīrāzī, pp. 25–26.

53 Shīrāzī, p. 27.

54 Juwaynī, vol. 3, pp. 253–260; Boyle, pp. 707–712; Rashīd al-Dīn, pp. 981–983.

> If there had not been such heavy rain that night, it was possible that they would have captured Rukn al-Dīn at the foot of the castle. Rukn al-Dīn became aware and in the morning went into the castle.[55]

The grip of the besieging army was tightened as troops from all directions converged in the manner of a *nerge*,[56] engulfing the whole area in less than 24 hours for six *farsangs* around the castle, so densely that a single man could not walk through those ranked soldiers.[57] Pestilence (*wabā*) is also credited with finally destroying the castle of Lamsar which the Khwarshāh's relatives held onto for more than a year, a fact which is not mentioned by Juwaynī. The warm reception which Hulegu afforded the young Rukn al-Dīn gladdened and encouraged him to call for the surrender of his remaining strongholds, most of which duly surrendered. The killing of Rukn al-Dīn on his trip east to Mongke's court, followed by the extermination of his extended family, his harem, and his retainers is reported coldly and factually without comment, in striking contrast to Juwaynī's exuberant version of events.[58]

The fall of Baghdad, 1258

The four short pages devoted to the fall of Baghdad contain one significant addition to the usual accounts of what has since been described both as a disastrous calamity for Islamic civilisation and as final liberation from Arab dominance. This is the role of pestilence in swelling the final death toll of Baghdad and revealing the use of the Tigris for the disposal of bodies. Otherwise the account of events leading up to the momentous confrontation between what has been depicted as the forces of good against the forces of evil, the battle between ancient foes, the Arabs and the Persians, or even the pitting of the steppe versus the sown, is here outlined and summarised in non-committed terms. No attempt is made to explain the civil war between Sunnis and Shi'ites that had been raging in the city and in its suburbs as well as the provinces. No reference is made to the destructive floods which had physically devastated the city the year before Hulegu's arrival.[59] However,

55 Shīrāzī, p. 28.
56 The Mongols' hunt described by many including Juwaynī, vol. 1, pp. 19–20; tr. Boyle, pp. 27–28; see George Lane, *Genghis Khan and Mongol Rule* (Westpoint: Greenwood, 2004), pp. 157–161.
57 Shīrāzī, p. 28.
58 Shīrāzī, p. 29.
59 On the fall of Baghdad see George Lane, "A Tale of Two Cities: The Fall of Hangzhou and Baghdad", *Central Asiatic Journal*, 2012/13, vol. 56, pp. 103–32; also Judith Pfeiffer, "Confessional Ambiguity vs. Confessional Polarization: Politics and the Negotiation of Religious Boundaries in the Ilkhanate", in *Politics, Patronage and the Transmission of Knowledge in 13th–15th Century Tabriz* (Leiden and Boston: Brill, 2013), pp. 129–168.

once again the author stresses the united front that the Iranian forces were able to present in the build up to the attack on Baghdad.

> From the province of Pars to the province of Rum, one body of men beyond borders and beyond number, descended on Baghdad.[60]

The position and role of each province's troops are then specified along with the position and role of Hulegu's top commanders and noyans, while the political intrigues and shenanigans which occupy so much space in other fuller accounts of this pivotal event are barely touched upon. Subtle differences between the words of Rashīd al-Dīn and "Shīrāzī's" account shape the readers' understanding of events. "Shīrāzī" describes "the armies of Pars and Kirman coming from the road of Khuzistan and Shishtar in such a way that their left hand came [along] the shores of the Omani sea"[61] whereas Rashīd al-Dīn refers to Ket Buqa Noyan, Qudsun, and Elgai entering "the left wing from Luristan, – , Khuzistan, and Bayat as far as the shore of the gulf."[62] "Shīrāzī" paints a picture of Persian armies massing and then moving towards Baghdad where Mongol commanders directed them into battle, whereas in Rashīd al-Dīn's account the emphasis is on the Mongol commanders and the fact that they had under their command Persian soldiery is almost ignored. Rashīd al-Dīn repeats certain details which suggest that he had access to and was willing to use parts of "Shīrāzī's" work, for example both accounts observe that when the supply of mangonel stones in Baghdad was exhausted, rocks were brought in from Jalula and Jabal Khamrin and then "date palms were cut down and hurled instead of stones."[63] What is interesting, however, is not what Rashīd al-Dīn copied, but rather what he possibly chose to ignore or to deliberately leave out.

Certain rather unedifying details are included such as the report of the dispatching of 12,000 ears belonging to the defeated army of the Caliph's *Dawātdār* (secretary of state) to Hulegu, the massacre of unarmed civilians after they had surrendered and gathered outside the city walls, the lack of space for burial of the dead compounded by the dearth of porters to dispose of the bodies, and the eventual donation by the Caliph of his own private grounds to be used for the burial of the growing numbers of putrefying corpses. The use of ears to verify the number of slain has a long history and is recorded by the European witnesses to the Mongol campaigns in Liegnitz and Eastern Europe with one account recording Batu being presented with

60 Shīrāzī, p. 30.
61 Shīrāzī, p. 30.
62 Rashid al-Dīn, p. 1012.
63 Rashid al-Dīn, p. 1013; Shīrāzī, p. 32.

nine sacks of ears.[64] The destruction of the city and citizens of Baghdad was caused, to a large extent, by the bombardment from massed mangonels, 16 to one 'tower', and their five to 100 *mann*[65] payloads. These awesome machines, "Persian Towers" (*Borj-e ᶜAjamī*), which had been erected by the Aleppo Gate and the Triumphant Gate, rained terror on the city, day and night, pulverising its battlements and defences.[66]

Most interesting, however, is the significance that the writer attributes to pestilence for swelling the reported numbers of the dead. Possibly because of his background in science, "Shīrāzī" seems more aware of the direct and indirect role that pestilence (*wabā*) played in warfare and especially its devastating effect on cities under siege. In Baghdad many people particularly the Sunnis, had flooded into the city from the suburbs and from Suwāb at the approach of the Mongols. Whereas the Shi'ites had come to an accommodation with Hulegu and their religious spokesman, Ibn Taᶜus, had pleased the new king with his fatwa endorsing the rule of a just infidel over an unjust Muslim,[67] the Sunnis were represented by the Caliph al-Mustaᶜṣim who had rejected all overtures for peace made by Hulegu.

> Pestilence struck and many people died. The number of deaths got to the point that the treasury's (*bayt al-māl*) priority was to provide the necessary equipment as well as burying the dead. Meanwhile it got to the point that they could not cope with ablutions and burying the dead so they threw the bodies into the Tigris. In the end it got so bad that they could not even carry the dead to the Tigris as the porters did not have time to even carry the corpses to the Tigris. At this point the Caliph ordered each area to assign an empty property in which to put the dead. When it became full they would carry them and as they got the opportunity they would bury them. Even when the army arrived they could not cope.[68]

Pestilence struck not only the citizens of Baghdad but their invaders as well, and the chronicle claims that a great many Mongols fell ill with the pestilence, that great numbers died, and that Hulegu Khan himself was amongst those struck down. However, after 20 days the Ilkhan recovered

64 See James Chambers, *The Devil's Horsemen* (London: Book Club Associates, 1979), p. 99.

65 1 *mann* = 3 kilos approx.

66 Shīrāzī, p. 32.

67 Ibn Ṭabāṭabā, *al-Fakhri: On the Systems of Government and the Muslim Dynasties*, tr. C.E.J. Whiting (London: Luzac & Co. Ltd., 1947); Muḥammad Alī bin Ṭabāṭabā (Ibn al-Ṭiqṭaqā), *Tārīkh-i Fakhrī*, tr. M.W. Gulpāygānī (Tehran: Be-negāh Tarjomeh va Nashr Ketāb, 1981/1360), p. 14.

68 Shīrāzī, p. 32.

and was able to spend the winter recuperating in Arran and Mughan, an episode ignored by Rashīd al-Dīn.[69]

The Caliph is awarded little space other than the final paragraph for the year 655 of the text and his slaughtered generals, even less. It is acknowledged that many civilians were murdered in cold blood by the invading forces despite the Caliph's surrender and his declaration of '*īl*' on their behalf. In fact many of those who had not accepted the promises of safe conduct from Hulegu's army and had hidden in the dark nooks and crannies, and even bath-stoves within the city, had survived. A couple of short sentences for the following year, 656, disposes of the Caliph and his family. Three words suffice for the Caliph himself, "*khalīfeh-rā shahīd kardand*" (They martyred the Caliph).[70] There is uncertainty whether the Caliph's two sons died before or after their father. The whole episode concludes with the observation that the warm weather that year caused a dreadful stench from the putrefaction prevailing in Baghdad. "Shīrāzī's" chronicle paints an incomplete and sketchy portrait of the besieged city but added to other far fuller accounts, it fills in some very important gaps and provides an independent and personal narrative with details not found elsewhere.

In fact, the traumatic impact of the fall of Baghdad and the collapse of the Caliphate seems to be more a later political construct and an added Arab narrative, devised in afterthought. Sa^cdī wrote some emotional verses and there is the famous oft quoted qaṡida by Taqī^c al-Dīn Ismā^cīl ibn abī al-Yusr[71] which is full of foreboding and lamentation but otherwise contemporary accounts are generally factual and unemotional. ^cAṭā Malek Juwaynī, an eye witness, chose not to record an account of the city's last days leaving that to his fellow courtier Naṣīr al-Dīn Ṭūsī whose brief summary of events became the definitive record, often attached to the end of Juwaynī's chronicle. Juwaynī finished his own history on an optimistic note with the fall of the blasphemous, heretical Ismailis and the advent of a new, far-sighted Great Khan, Mongke, and with a new Iranian king and dynasty under Hulegu, headed by a fresh generation of advisers and courtiers made up of Persians, many of them Muslims and traditionalists like him.[72] He also did not wish to commit to paper his own views on the fall of Baghdad and the Caliphate, and on the rule of the Arab Abbasids and their administration, since he was soon to become governor of the city himself and he came from a family

69 Shīrāzī, p. 34.
70 Shīrāzī, p. 34.
71 Joseph de Somogyi, "A Qasida on the Destruction of Baghdad by the Mongols", *BSOAS*, Vol. 7, No.1 (1933), pp. 41–48.
72 Juwaynī, Boyle, p. 638; Qazvīnī, pp. 138–139.

of canny and experienced politicians who understood the implications of a careless remark, ambiguous conclusion, or an inappropriate sound-bite.

Hulegu's remit from his brother, Mongke, upon leaving Qaraqorum for Iran was not to destroy the ruling administration in Baghdad but more to invite them to submit and enjoy his grace and patronage. The Caliph al-Mustaᶜṣim had chosen to harken to the advice of his warring councillors, who had their own agendas and who represented rival factions of Iraq's suicidal civil war. The Caliph is universally portrayed as a weak and indecisive man more interested in music and the pleasures of life than in the machinations and intrigues of palace politics. Even Hulegu is shocked by the indecisiveness of the Caliph when he eventually has him before his throne. "What kind of man are you, and what intellect and experience of affairs (tadbīr) do you possess, that you neither gathered an army to confront us, nor pursued (a policy of) graciousness and moderation with us?"[73] A neighbour of the Caliph and reluctant ally of Hulegu, the Kurdish warlord and governor of Mosul and Irbil, Badr al-Dīn Lu'lu (d.1259), provided an apt anecdote regarding the Caliph. As Hulegu made his relentless journey westward, he sent Lu'lu a message telling him to send men and armaments to him urgently. At the same time Lu'lu also received a message from the Caliph, fretting in his palace. The Caliph was in desperate need of musicians and appealed to Lu'lu to help him. Lu'lu's comment, "Look at the two requests, and weep for Islam and its people."[74] Badr al-Dīn Lu'lu remained in power until his death and his actions saw both Mosul and Irbil escape the destruction which overtook other cities in the region.

Hulegu had been welcomed by the Iranians and the ranks of his army had been swelled by the addition of troops from Iran's city-states. Hulegu had also been welcomed by the Kurdish warlords in the west and the Arab Shi'ites from Iraq whose representative at the Caliph's court, the minister, Ibn al-ᶜAlqamī, had already been in correspondence with Hulegu. The Shi'ite community's leader, Ibn Taᶜus, had secured protection for his community and their holy sites and Waṣṣāf reports that the Shi'ite clerics assured Hulegu that their scriptures had foretold his arrival and that Alī ibn Abī Ṭālib himself had said that "you [Hulegu] will one day be the owners of this land, that the grip of your power will defeat its governor."[75] In Iran, the Sunni clergy had already expressed their own support for Hulegu, and the leader of the delegation which had originally travelled to Mongke's coronation had been the Sunni Qadi of Qazvin. Later the highly respected Iranian

73 From The *Tuḥfeh* for Atabeg Aḥmad of Luristan translated by Louise Marlowe; Moḥammad Taqī Danishpazhuh (ed.), *Tuḥfeh* (Tehran: B.T.N.K., 1962/1341), p. 216.

74 Ibn Ṭiqṭaqā (Ṭabāṭabā), *Tārīkh-i-Fakhrī* (London: Luzac, 1946).

75 Waṣṣāf, p. 36; translation, 117.

Sunni theologian, ᶜAbdullāh Bayḍāwī, published a small historical pamphlet of immense symbolic importance, the *Niżām al-tavārīkh*, which officially recognised the Ilkhanate as an authentic, legitimate Iranian dynasty.[76]

Hulegu ordered the clean-up and opening of the bazaars shortly after the execution of the Caliph and his sons. The destruction in the city had been exaggerated and first-hand accounts of the assault suggest the devastation and the killing was often discretionary. Arrows were shot into the city assuring Christians, Shi'ites, and non-combatants safe passage. The famous musician ᶜUrmawī invited the commander Bayju Noyan to a feast and entertainment and so ensured not only that his own district escaped harm but also that he was employed as a court musician for Hulegu after hostilities had ceased. Certainly, destruction was selective and the houses and places of worship of 'friends' and allies were spared, including the property of merchants who had already established contacts with the conquering forces. "So when Baghdad was conquered, [these merchants] went to the emirs and returned with guards to secure their homes."[77] The Caliph's top generals and ministers were executed despite some of them having been promised a reprieve. His own generals had recognised the danger of having a number of influential, powerful and disgruntled military commanders loose in the crippled city. At least one son of the Caliph escaped with his life and was sent in servitude to Mongolia, and a daughter was married to Harūn, a son of Juwaynī and a governor of Anatolia. A relative of al-Mustaᶜṣim appeared in Cairo and founded the discredited Abbasid Caliphate of Cairo which was recognised by few if any outside of the Mamluk's territories.

The city's clean-up was put in the hands of locals, directed by among others, Ibn al-ᶜAlqamī, who, had he been suspected of treachery against his late master, the Caliph, would certainly have been executed by Hulegu as disloyal and untrustworthy. Instead the World Conqueror is recorded as having observed, "'He is an intelligent man; he attends both to our interests and to those of his own master'"[78] The former finance minister, al-Dāmghānī, also served Hulegu in Baghdad but eventually the post went to ᶜAṭā Malek Juwaynī, whose brother Shams al-Dīn was appointed Ṣāḥib Dīvān of the Ilkhanate, an extremely powerful and influential position.

76 See Charles Melville, "From Adam to Abaqa: Qadi Baidawi's Rearrangement of History (Part I)", *Studia Iranica*, Vol. 30, No. 1 (2001), pp. 67–86; "From Adam to Abaqa: Qadi Baidawi's Rearrangement of History (Part II)", *Studia Iranica*, Vol. 36, No. 1 (2007), pp. 7–64 [reprinted with Persian trans. together with part I, by Mohammad Reza Tahmasbi, Tehran 2008].

77 Hend Gilly-Elewy, "Al-Ḥawādit al-ğāmiʿa: A Contemporary Account of the Mongol Conquest of Baghdad, 656/1258", *Arabica*, Vol. 58 (2011), pp. 353–371, 367.

78 From The *Tuḥfeh* for Atabeg Aḥmad of Luristan translated by Louise Marlowe; Moḥammad Taqī Danishpazhuh, p. 217.

Figure 1.5 Merchants, Hangzhou

"Persian merchants and adventurers traversed the mountains and valleys of all the lands conquered by the Chinggisid armies as celebrated in this delicate rock carving from the hills overlooking Hangzhou's West Lake in China."

[ch.1, p. 25] Photo by author

While Baghdad slowly recovered from its many years of civil war, natural calamities, and its latest travails, Hulegu continued his advance into Syria and Palestine.[79]

The conquest of Syria

As mentioned earlier, "Shīrāzī's" chronicle does not share the antipathy felt towards the Ismailis that is commonly found in the works of Sunni commentators. The standard offensive epithets for the Ismailis such as *mulahida* [heretic] are used routinely in many chronicles, but the author

79 On post-invasion Baghdad see Weissmann, PhD dissertation.

perhaps reveals the true direction of his sympathies later when discussing the appointment of Shi'ite governors to Damascus. This incident occurs in the year 657 following the death of the Caliph in 656 (1258). The conquest of Syria is dealt with summarily with Aleppo, which endured a massacre, contrasted with Damascus, which escaped the former's fate after having sent envoys to Hulegu bearing gifts. Rashīd al-Dīn explains the background to the welcome laid out for Hulegu by the grandees of Damascus and the two accounts agree on at least the names of the two Persian governors appointed to the city, ᶜAlā al-Dīn Jāstī and Qādī Shams al-Dīn Qumī, though Rashīd al-Dīn names another Persian governor, Jamāl al-Dīn Qaraqāī Qazvīnī, and claims that a Mongol *shahna* was also sent to oversee the three Tajiks [Iranians].[80] "Shīrāzī's" account comments on the surprisingly warm welcome afforded the envoys from the people of Damascus, explaining first that the two Persians were Shi'ites from the holy city of Qom. "Shīrāzī" is 'amazed' that the two 'Shi'a-ye Qumī' were greeted so warmly and that no adverse incidents or emotions emerged during their tenure. However, what marks this passage as significant is the epithet used by the author to describe the people of Damascus. "Shīrāzī" states that "most people in Damascus are Yazīdī"[81] a reference to the second Umayyad Caliph Yazīd ibn Muᶜāwiya ibn Abī Sufyān (645–683CE/60–63 AH) who is held in contempt by all Muslims but who is particularly hated by the Shi'ites, who hold him responsible for the murder of Imam Husein bin 'Alī. Referring to Sunnis as Yazidis would be considered both provocative and insulting, and its use here also suggests that the audience for this chronicle might have been limited or restricted to non-Sunnis. The acknowledged presence of the chronicle in Rashīd al-Dīn's library is therefore noteworthy.

Battle of ᶜAyn Jalūt

Both the Mamluks and the beginnings of the conflict with the Qipchaq Khanate are briefly dealt with in the entries for the year 658, once again with chance remarks providing important insight into the development of the Ilkhanate. The year 658 opens with a eulogy to Ket Buqa who is described as being the *modār*, the pivot, the central cog of the army while acknowledging that at the same time there were in fact amirs and other officers of greater and higher rank than he. Ket Buqa's demise is acknowledged as signalling the end of Mongol signature military victories, "*ba'd az u lashgār-i*

80 Rashid al-Dīn, p. 1027. The term 'Tajik' is often used to describe Persians and Iranians in general.
81 Shīrāzī, p. 35.

moghūl-rā beh hīch jāneb-i fathī [unreadable] *etafāq niyoftāb*"[82] and indeed the Battle of ᶜAyn Jalūt on 3rd September 1260/658 though militarily of no great consequence, had profound symbolic significance which was recognised by "Shīrāzī." The battle was considered a victory against the Chinggisids not only by the Mamluks but by the Syrian Franks and their cousins in Europe which would explain the hesistancy on the part of the Pope to form an alliance with the Mongols.[83] Rashīd al-Dīn describes the battle in considerably more detail, along with Ket Buqa's last stand and his brave last words before his death at the command of the Mamluk Quduz. "Shīrāzī" includes a short exchange between Ket Buqa and the amir, Bāydar, who retreated before Quduz to await the arrival of his commander. Ket Buqa demands to know why he had not stood his ground and died defending that ground. Bāydar admits that he had been unable to but questions Ket Buqa's ability or willingness to make the ultimate sacrifice.[84] The following day at dawn those of the Ilkhanid army who had stood their ground were killed, while the remnants of the small troop including Ket Buqa himself were chased down and massacred on the banks of the river 'Āsī near the Syrian town of Homs. Ket Buqa's wives, sons, and concubines were captured in Ba'lbak. "Shīrāzī's" report of the Battle of ᶜAyn Jalūt is followed by a short account of the succession of Rukn al-Dīn Bunduqdar Baybars to the Egyptian throne in which he explicitly accuses the Mamluk sultan of murdering his predecessor. He considers Baybars to be unique and his judgement and order (*rāī va tartīb*) unrivalled, exemplified in the Sultan's first edicts forbidding wine and also forbidding assembly and consultation between grandees – especially between the military and the Turks.[85]

Rashīd al-Dīn makes no reference to any of this, dwelling instead on Ket Buqa's final moments. In Rashīd al-Dīn's account the Mamluk sultan upbraids the Mongol general's pride, accusing the Mongols of relying on magic and artifice, "Speak not so proudly of the horsemen of Turan, for they perform deeds with trickery and artifice, not with manliness like Rustam." "*Kār-hā-ye beh nīrang va dastān mīkonand.*"[86] The word *nīrang* has connotations of miracles, sorcery, and otherworldiness and it brings to mind the Mamluks[87] rebuking the Ottomans for their use of firearms and the Polish

82 Shīrāzī, p. 36.

83 See Peter Jackson, *The Mongols and the Islamic World* (New Haven and London: Yale University Press, 2017), pp. 132–133.

84 Shīrāzī, pp. 36–37.

85 Shīrāzī, p. 37.

86 Rashīd al-Dīn, 1994, p. 1033.

87 The Mamluks ruled from Cairo from 1250–1382 (Baḥrī) and 1382–1517 (Burjī). The Mamluks were a military government of 'slave' soldiers, the majority of whom originated

accusations of magic and sorcery when they witnessed the Mongols' use of explosives. "Shīrāzī" does not recount this exchange but when he reports the use of subterfuge and deception by the Franks in the following story, the word he employs is *ḥiylat kārī* [trickery, deceit] rather than *nīrang*.

Seven-hundred Franks appeared before the Muslims, though names, dates, and places are not specified, and claimed that in a dream they had become Muslims and that in their hearts they feared the religion and faith of the Franks. They had come to offer their service to the sultan [*beh khidmat-i sultān āmadeh 'īm*] so that they [the Muslims] might present to them the religion of Islam and teach them in a school in order that they could learn the Qoran. The Franks wished to have a *waqf* created to cover their instruction in the Sunna and the Shari'ah. They planned to gain the Muslims' trust and then during 'Eid Qorban when "all Muslims would be outside and standing in prayer they could put hand to sword and strike down the Musselman."[88] However Bunduqdar's suspicions were aroused and he ordered the men seized and their persons inspected. It was soon discovered that beneath their clothes they were wearing jerkins and chain mail and each man possessed a small sword of fine Damascus steel [*nīmcheh-ye ābdār*]. The story had a satisfactory ending with prayers met and wishes granted. The Franks were bound and carried to the square for public prayer and then their request for instruction in the rites of Islam was granted. "Tell them, first you must learn to stand for prayer. Then we will teach you the *qurbān*, the sacrifice."[89] When the congregation of Muslims had prayed, the Franks were ordered to be prepared in the manner of a sacrificial animal and their throats were cut with a knife in the same way as an animal was sacrificed. When their clothes were removed all of them were seen to be wearing the finest jerkins and the finest chain mail and the congregation realised the true nature of their guests. From that time on great fear was instilled in the hearts of the Franks and on the few occasions when Hulegu sent his armies into Syria, the Franks did not respond.[90]

The Christian Armenians, especially those from Cilicia whose capital was the fortified city of Sis, the ruins of which lie close to today's regional capital, Adana, maintained excellent relations with the new Ilkhanid regime just as they had with successive Chinggisid rulers, local, regional, and central. King Hetoum had accompanied Hulegu back from Mongke's coronation. The castle of Sis was significantly enlarged in the thirteenth century during the reigns of King Levon I and King Hetoum I with a 'palace,' residential

---

from the Caucasus, Qipchaq Khanate, and the Eurasian steppe, including Mongols but who also included eastern Europeans and other diverse ethnicities.

88 Shīrāzī, pp. 37–38.

89 Shīrāzī, p. 37.

90 Shīrāzī, p. 39.

buildings, churches, and gardens and in 1241, Hetoum's wife, Zapēl, constructed a hospital in what had become a fully functioning capital city. "Hetoum" is mentioned in a fragment of a dedicatory inscription extant within the castle ruins.[91] After the fall of the castle of Hromkla (Rum Kala) to the Mamluks, Sis became the Catholicos' residence though in 1266 the Egyptians burnt and pillaged the city, as recorded by Grigor of Akner in his chronicle, the *Nation of Archers*.

> They burned the town of Sis, which was the seat of the Armenian kings. They cast wood into the fire and great church which was the centre of Sis and they burned it. They demolished the tombs of the kings.[92]

Whereas the relationship with the Armenians from the Caucasus had not been normalised until the advent of Hulegu circa 1256, the Armenian Cilicians had remained staunch allies and apologists for the Chinggisids. They defended and propagated the Chinggisid cause in Rome and among the Franks with whom these Eastern Christians did not always enjoy the best of relations. Relations with the Caucasian Armenians improved after some of their leading clerics entered the Ilkhanid administration as functionaries. Negotiations were led by polymath and celebrated historian, Vardan Arewelts'i (1198–1271, the "Easterner"), who later became a confessor and private, spiritual adviser to Hulegu's wife, Dokuz Khatun.

The Jochid princes

It was in the north with his cousins rather than the south with the Franks or the Mamluks that Hulegu found himself most dangerously embroiled. The fate of three Jochid princes, Bulghāī, Tūtār, and Tūlī, complicated an already tense situation upon which "Shīrāzī" fails to throw new light.[93] Prince Berke, whose brother, Batu, had died shortly before the attack on Baghdad, openly challenged the legitimacy of Hulegu's presence in Iran and instigated verbal and military hostilities. Both Hulegu and his brother, the Great Khan Qubilai, had opposed Berke's claim to the Jochid throne and Berke in turn had backed Ariq Buqa's challenge to his older brother, Qubilai, for the Qa'anate throne itself. "Shīrāzī" explicitly states Berke's position as regards Iran. "Berke's shahnas and governors and his people had the finest

91 See Robert W. Edwards, "The Fortifications of Cilician Armenia", *Dumbarton Oaks Studies*, Vol. 23 (1987), pp. 233–237, pls.211a–221a.

92 Translated Robert Bedrosian, attributed to Grigor of Akner *History of the Nation of Archers*, p.356, <www.attalus.org/armenian/gatoc.html>. Last accessed 31 May 2017.

93 Shīrāzī, pp. 39, 41.

Figure 1.6 Mediaeval Tblisi; close up of a public display in the centre of Old Tblisi (Sketch by Sir William Simpson, The Illustrated London News, 9th June, 1888)

The Caucasus was coveted by all the Chinggisid Khans and Berke's agents laid claim to many of the cities and towns of the region, the scene of many violent encounters. Tblisi's Kura river was a bitterly fought over boundary.

Photo by author

and the best of the choice provinces of Khorasan, Iraq, Azerbaijan. Arran, Georgia, and they claimed that our special land was their *inju* [land]."[94] While failing to add anything new regarding the fate of the Jochid princes, "Shīrāzī" provides important new context for the hostilities which grew into an intractable split between the two cousins and neighbours. He makes it clear that the Jochids continued to treat parts of Iran as their own just as they had from the original invasions in the 1220s and that this arrogance was resented by the rest of Hulegu's noyans and commanders. Berke considered his own rights in Transcaucasia equal if not greater than Hulegu's and the episode with the princes was a convenient *casus bello*.

The seeds of conflict between the House of Tolui and the House of Jochi had first been sown with the fateful reference to the tread of Tatar hoof. The gestation and growth of that dispute during the lifetime of Batu is covered

94 Shīrāzī, p. 40.

in various chronicles but it was the death of Mongke, the controversy of Qubilai's assumption of the Qa'an's throne, and the rise of Berke following his brother, Batu's demise which ignited the fuse of war. The Mamluk historians Ibn Shaddād and al-ᶜUmarī and the Armenian sources provide details lacking in the Persian Toluid sources though Rashīd al-Dīn is able to provide evidence of the ill-feeling, rivalry, and perceived disrespect which existed in the relationship between Hulegu and Berke.[95] Once the fate of the princes became known, Jochid loyalists deserted Hulegu's army and fled north to the Caucasus, south to the haven offered by the Mamluks or east following the commander Negudar who eventually settled in the wildlands of the Hindu Kush south of Bactria where he made contact with other Jochid loyalists including troops under the command of Sali Noyan. The Negudārīs joined forces with these essentially autonomous troops and the army, which had once campaigned in India and who served as a buffer between the Delhi Sultanate and the Ilkhanate, soon became infamous as the Qara'unas. The Qara'unas were an outlaw, mercenary armed element who are believed to be the ancestors of the Hazaras of central Afghanistan. "Shīrāzī" acknowledges their involvement in the hostilities between Ahmad Tegudar and Arghun Khan but appears non-committal, treating them as just another armed element. The Qara'unas had become a major irritant after they launched a raid into Fars and Kirman in 677/1278–9, provoking a response from Abaqa the following year. He forced their submission and he even drafted some of them into Ilkhanid service in central and western Iran, but the bulk of their forces returned to a more subdued version of their former ways.[96]

The depth of the split between Hulegu and Berke was dramatically increased when Berke officially allied himself with the Mamluks against his cousin and neighbour. Although inter-Mongol rivalry, open hostility, and military clashes were nothing new among the Chinggisids, alliances with outsiders against another Mongol prince were and Berke's willingness to take this treacherous step solidified the split which had already riven the Chinggisid. Berke already had solid economic ties with Cairo, but now he added the cement of Islam and declared Jihad against the infidel slayers of the Caliph and the occupiers of Muslim lands and cities. War was declared.

Jalāl al-Dīn, son of the late *dawātdār*

The story of Jalāl al-Dīn, the son of Baghdad's *dawātdār*, is another episode found in other accounts of the time but again the significance of "Shīrāzī's" account is not in the narrative shared with the other histories and chronicles

95 For an overview see Jackson, 2017, pp. 141–148; Rashid al-Dīn, pp. 362, 511.
96 See Rashīd al-Dīn, pp. 772, 1109–1110, 1210–1211.

but rather those details which the other accounts chose to ignore. The dashing figure of Jalāl al-Dīn is dealt with in the entries for the years 656/1258 and 662/1264. He immediately brings to mind another Jalāl al-Dīn who was also a controversial and ambiguous figure who excited passion and conflicting reaction. For Juwaynī, Jalāl al-Dīn Mingburnu Khwārazmshāh was the romantic symbol of Persian bravery and steadfastness standing against the irresistible tide of Turanian brutality,[97] though for most observers, contemporary and current, the final Khwārazmshāh was a duplicitous bandit, a cruel tyrant, a drunken killer, and a merciless hypocrite who fully deserved his fate on a lonely Kurdish hilltop in 1231. There, after years of "leaping all over Iran like a stag",[98] he was waylaid and murdered by Kurdish bandits for his fine clothes.[99] Juwaynī's indulgent and excessive homily to this dangerous fugitive is not easily explained. Neither too is Hulegu's blind attraction to another Jalāl al-Dīn, the dashing young courtier whose once powerful father, the chamberlain Aybek, had recently been executed on the Ilkhan's orders. It was this Jalāl al-Dīn in "Shīrāzī's" chronicle who survived the fate of his father, the lesser *dawātdār* of the Caliph al-Musta'ṣim, only to be very publicly awarded a position of great trust and access under Hulegu Khan, much to the consternation and resentment of others in the court.

Hulegu had been humiliated by Berke after his disastrous adventure in the Caucasus where, according to "Shīrāzī", his armies had suffered a serious defeat. In "Shīrāzī's" account, Hulegu's reaction to this defeat is emphasised and the subject of his health is once again mentioned. He felt such great stress that he became sick and every time he began to recover the same stressful thoughts would return until he suffered a relapse and his sickness would recur.

It was while Hulegu was nursing his wounds and contemplating the form his retaliation against Berke should take that he heard reports of the young Jalāl al-Dīn. According to "Shīrāzī", there was no one spoken of so highly and graciously as he in all Hulegu's lands or in his armies. Jalāl al-Dīn claimed that in the Caliph's domains at that time, there were several thousand Qipchaq Turks who were intimately acquainted with the land and the culture [*shīveh*] of the Qipchaq steppes. He then offered to assemble these Turks and to lead them into battle against Berke's armies which still occupied the strategically and politically important Caucasus. Much to the discomfort of the Perso-Mongol elite, Jalāl al-Dīn was firstly given the ear of the king whom he advised on the sensitive issue of the Jochid princes and was secondly given sweeping powers to assemble his own armies and

97 Juwaynī, Qazvīnī, vol. 2, pp. 126–201; tr. Boyle, pp. 396–468.

98 As the Syriac polymath and cleric, Bar Hebraeus, described him.

99 Juwaynī, Qazvīnī, vol. 2, pp. 190–192; tr. Boyle, pp. 459–460.

supplies with the full cooperation of all and without interference from anyone.[100] Jalāl al-Dīn arrived in Baghdad in 662/1264 and he struck everyone as a man with a mission. In secret he told his troops that the king had sent him to recruit men for the frontline "who would die there or who would make a name for themselves. If you are killed in that place, in your place, you others will continue the very same work."[101] The wording is close enough to that found in Rashīd al-Dīn to presume either a common shared source or possibly that Shīrāzī is Rashīd al-Dīn's source. Jalāl al-Dīn continues, "Now you all know who I am and whose son I am and that I would not allow you to become sword fodder for the infidel." He reveals that Hulegu had been admonishing him and he now wanted to "abandon this state and fortune of the infidels . . . let us cast ourselves away from the hand of the Mongols."[102] To the roll of drums Jalāl al-Dīn led his army across the bridge and away from Baghdad, raided the Khafāja Arabs for plunder including a few camels and a few buffalo and with supplies from Baghdad's treasuries he announced his intentions of visiting the holy shrines but his true plans and destination were soon made plain to his troops.

He then famously betrayed that great trust placed in him by Hulegu and defected to the Mamluks with many of the men under his command. However, "Shīrāzī's" account invests the whole incident with far greater significance than it is given elsewhere and suggests that Hulegu suffered deeply from this betrayal, "wringing his hands and gnashing his teeth",[103] so much so that he became gravely ill with a malady which defied the treatment and knowledge of a variety of doctors. Yet again "Shīrāzī", who had seen Hulegu in person on many occasions, focuses on Hulegu's health and his mental state in particular. The account quotes the anguished Hulegu who, it suggests, regarded the young Jalāl al-Dīn as almost a son, as crying: 'a child cannot play with me like this.' There is even the hint that by immediately following the report of this incident with the account of the Ilkhan's death on the banks of the river Jaghatu in 663/1265, that Hulegu never recovered from the trauma and died soon afterwards.

Rashīd al-Dīn recounts this same incident,[104] though he mentions only that it left the king furious. It is likely that the *Akhbār* was the source or alternatively that there was another shared source for this story. Both accounts refer to Hulegu using the men as 'sword fodder' [*alof-i-shamshīr*] and both repeat Jalāl al-Dīn's incitement to cast off the 'Mongol yoke' [*dast-i-īn Moghūlān bīrūn afkonam*] and the two accounts both refer dismissively

100 Shīrāzī, p. 41.
101 Shīrāzī, p. 42.
102 Shīrāzī, p. 42.
103 Shīrāzī, p. 43.
104 Rashid al-Dīn, pp. 1049–1051.

to Jalāl al-Dīn's diversionary attacks on the Khafāja Arabs. A decision must have been taken at the *Rab' al-Rashīdī*[105] in Tabriz to reject the details of Hulegu's severe reaction to the treachery.

The comparatively few extant pages given to Abaqa Khan's reign are concerned chiefly with the conspiracy against the Juwaynī brothers, though some space is also given to the Mamluk invasion of Anatolia and the fate of the Parvana of the Saljuq Sultanate of Rum. The Saljuq Sultanate of Rum, which had always enjoyed independence from the empire of the Great Saljuqs whose last sultan had fallen to the sword of their one-time vassal, the Khwarazmshah Tekish [r.1172–1200], had submitted to the Chinggisid armies of Bayju Noyan in 1243 after the battle of Köse Dağ. They had maintained their capital in Konya and had continued to be a magnet for cultural, spiritual, and even political dissidents from much of the Islamic world, though their topography and climate also attracted Turkoman nomads from the Eurasian steppe. Though the Sultan remained on his throne, political power lay with a Chinggisid appointee, Mu'īn al-Dīn Parvana [r.1243–77], who originally hailed from Kashan in central Iran.

In 675/1276 Baybars Bunduqdar brought his army to Rum where at Āblastān he confronted the Ilkhanid army commanded by the grand amirs Tūqū bin Alkāī and Tūdavān bin Sodūn. The Ilkhanid army suffered a defeat and the two amirs were killed. Rashīd al-Dīn covers these events but in far more detail than the *Akhbār* and with slight variations which suggest that the two accounts are completely independent.[106] Both accounts have Baybars to whom they both refer as either Bunduqdar or Rukn al-Dīn Bunduqdar, occupying Kayseri for a week and his armies suffering deprivation as a result of his strict discipline, restrictions on expenditure '*nafqeh barīshān tang shod*'[107] and orders forbidding looting and pillaging of the country. He called on Mu'īn al-Dīn, the Parvana, to attend him at court offering the governor of the Ilkhanid-dominated Saljuq Sultanate of Rum, the kingship of Rum if he would overcome his fear of the Mongols and come to Kayseri. "Shīrāzī" reports only that the Parvana failed to go to Bunduqdar's court and the Mamluk sultan eventually abandoned his short-lived occupation and left Anatolia.

105 This was the complex in Tabriz founded by Rashīd al-Dīn which contained his library, madressa, lecture halls, presses, and studios. Through Bolad Shingsang the institute was twinned with a similar seat of learning in the Yuan capital, Khanbaliq/Dadu [Beijing], the Hanlin academy. W.A.P. Martin, "The Hanlin Yuan", *The North American Review*, Vol. 119, No. 244 (July, 1874), pp. 1–33; Abolala Soudavar, "The Han-Lin Academy and the Persian Royal Library-Atelier", in Judith Pfeiffer and Sholeh A. Quinn (eds.), *History and Historiography of Post-Mongol Central Asia and the Middle East: Studies in Honour of John E. Woods* (Wiesbaden: Harrassowitz, 2006), pp. 467–483.

106 Rashīd al-Dīn, pp. 1101–1102.

107 Shīrāzī, p. 48.

"Shīrāzī" makes no mention of the rumours sown by the frustrated Mamluk ruler of Mu'īn al-Dīn's treachery, nor of his execution on Abaqa's orders, nor of the dreadful claim made by Armenian chroniclers that he was ordered eaten by his Ilkhanid jailers.[108] Eventually Abaqa himself marched on Syria and, after appointing his brother commander, he dispatched Prince Mongke Temur, son of Ulja Khatun, along the Diyarbakir road in the direction of Syria. Mongke Temur encountered the Mamluk army in the vicinity of Homs and Hama and the two armies clashed after which the young and inexperienced Mongke Temur suffered an 'ugly' defeat. Abaqa Khan was so angry at Mongke Temur's ignominious rout that, "Shīrāzī" claims, he could not look his brother in the face. The Ilkhan announced that he did not view the situation as problematic and that the following year he himself would go to Syria "to see what could be done."[109] That winter Abaqa remained in Baghdad. "Shīrāzī's" last word on this matter is the observation that Bunduqdar died during these events and that the throne was passed to Malek Alfī, "a Qipchaq (*Qifjāq*) who was also a slave of the sultans of Syria that is the people of Salah al-Dīn,"[110] al-Malik al-Sa'īd Nāṣir al-Dīn Barakah [1277–79].

The Juwaynī brothers[111]

The travails of the Juwaynī brothers occupy the rest of the entry for 675/1277 and the sole topic for the entry for the year 679/1280, the intervening years remaining unrecorded by "Shīrāzī". Once again, the repetition of small snatches of the narrative and use of common phrases suggests that "Shīrāzī" was Rashīd al-Dīn's source or that again the two shared a common source. "Shīrāzī" claims that ᶜAlā al-Dīn was arrested, his property confiscated, his palaces and houses pillaged, and he himself placed in the cangue. This had come about after the wily Majd al-Mulk had forced himself into the king's presence (*beh khidmat-i-Abaqa andākhteh*)[112] to make his accusations which had then been compounded by the smears and attacks of 40 or 50 writers and notables. Once started, the campaign gathered pace and the Juwaynīs were abandoned and it is their isolation that "Shīrāzī" stresses. Hamdallāh Mustawfī Qazvīnī fleetingly covers these events though he does not dwell on the details. What makes Mustawfī's account noteworthy is his

108 Hetoum, *A Lytell Cronycle*, ed. Glenn Burger (Toronto: University of Toronto Press, 1988), p. 46.
109 Shīrāzī, p. 49.
110 Shīrāzī, p. 49.
111 See George Lane, "Jovayni, ᶜAlā al-Din", *Encyclopaedia Iranica*, <www.iranicaonline.org/articles/jovayni-ala-al-din> Accessed 1 June 2017.
112 Shīrāzī, p. 49.

obvious high regard for Majd al-Mulk, who is elsewhere treated, at best, neutrally. While acknowledging the misfortune that Majd al-Mulk caused Shams al-Dīn, whose Juwayn-based family were, of cause, fierce rivals of the Qazvin-based family of the generally objective and highly respected historian, Mustawfī's sentiments are made clear: "There was a man of Yazd who was wise, liberal, and eloquent, full of knowledge and nobly born . . . on the 20th *Jammadī avval* that great man met destruction."[113]

It is unclear exactly when these events surrounding Aṭā Malik took place since the year 675/1277 under which Īraj Afshār, the editor, places them is clearly too early. A later entry for 679/1280 referring to Majd al-Mulk's audience with Abaqa in the public disrobing room of the bath-house (*moslikh-i-garmāveh*) of the *Ribat-i Musallim* opens with the words "To continue . . . in the season of spring of the year 679/1280" which suggests more realistically that these tumultuous events occurred around the later part of 678/1279, which would agree with Rashīd al-Dīn's account even though the two versions differ substantially in the detail. Though the two Juwaynī brothers were fearful and extremely downcast, 'broken' (*shekasteh shodand*) in "Shīrāzī's" words, Shams al-Dīn did not show any outward sign of this and his inner turmoil was not apparent. Summoned from Baghdad, he was confronted in Siyāh Kuh and ordered to surrender all the money and material (*māl*) he had taken from the king. It was his former colleague, his nawāb, Majd al-Dīn ibn Athīr, who confronted him demanding that he reveal what he had obtained from "such and such a person and from such and such a place."[114]

"Shīrāzī" and Rashīd al-Dīn, in almost identical words, record Shams al-Dīn advising his brother not to deny anything until forced to do so, "*beh hīch bāb (vajeh) ankār makon ke (tā) tu-rā be-ranjānand (zaḥmatī naresad).*"[115] "Shīrāzī" adds that the 'money' is not worth the loss of honour while both commentators agree that 'Aṭā Malik was forced to pay three million pieces of gold. "Shīrāzī" concludes his account of the unfortunate minister with the observation that before Abaqa's death in 680/1281, ᶜAṭā Malik was further mulcted on which development Rashīd al-Dīn elaborates with the claim that the fallen minister was forced to sell everything he had, including his sons, and "he lost everything as Majd al-Mulk's fortunes rose."[116]

Majd al-Mulk's own personal triumph finds similar treatment in both sources and once again the wording is almost identical, with Abaqa in

113 Ḥamdullah Mustawfī, *Ẓafarnāma* (Tehran: University of Tehran, 1999), p. 1288; L. J. Ward (tr.), *The Zafarnamah of Mustawfī*, PhD Thesis, University of Manchester, 1983, pp. 262, 269. Initially, Majd al-Mulk is mistakenly referred to as Majd al-Dīn.

114 Shīrāzī, p. 50; Rashīd al-Dīn, p. 1115.

115 Shīrāzī, p. 50; Rashīd al-Dīn (bracketed), p. 1115.

116 Rashīd al-Dīn, p. 1115.

Maragha's Buddhist temple in the presence of all his relatives, nobles, wives, ministers, and amirs, ordering the public proclamation of his edict concerning Majd al-Mulk. "Mongol kings had never before granted anyone [a Tajik] such a *yarlīgh*."[117] "Shīrāzī" quotes more from the edict than Rashīd al-Dīn but both convey the significance of the decision and its implications for the Juwaynīs. "Shīrāzī's" account has Abaqa being far more extreme in his regard for Majd al-Mulk. The king declared his kingdom, his property, the treasury, his flocks, all that he possessed should henceforth be shared with Majd al-Mulk, and that their duties would be borne by the minister and his deputies (*nawāb*), "those who are friends of you are my friends. After this if a person should plot against you, I will be with you." He urged the minister to take care of himself and never to leave him. "Shīrāzī's" account of this incident suggests that Abaqa Khan's behaviour is extremely eccentric, whereas Rashīd al-Dīn dilutes the hyperbole and modifies the context. Reactions to Abaqa's extraordinary edict were predictable with all the amirs and notables switching sides and deferring to the newly promoted minister, Majd al-Mulk, whose deputies were immediately dispatched to oversee the notables and tax districts of all the "provinces from inside Rum to the ends of Khorasan, from the deserts of Arabia to Darband of Saqsīn."[118] In obvious admiration "Shīrāzī" notes that in one particular project Majd al-Mulk "raised an edifice" the likes of which no one could remember and "in the space of seven or eight months somebody who had been of no account anywhere should manage a project of such magnitude."[119] Though he is generally portrayed in a negative light, in "Shīrāzī's" account Majd al-Mulk surprisingly accrues some credit with the acknowledgement that his achievements amazed "every living creature."[120] "Shīrāzī" delivers a balanced account of one of the most emotive events in Ilkhanid history, a story from which nobody emerged untainted or blamefree. In any final analysis or conclusive summary of "Shīrāzī", his stance on the plight of the Juwaynīs must hold some significance.

Two brief entries are recorded for 680/1281 and 681/1282 outlining Abaqa's infamous end from an excess of alcohol. Though Abaqa enjoyed almost universal 'good press', all also acknowledge his excessive attachment to drinking. "The mighty shah entered into pleasures and was not separated for a moment from drinking."[121] There is a suggestion that the king fell drunkenly from a lavatory (*kursī*), a rare reference to such a utensil,[122] after having

117 Shīrāzī, p. 51; Rashīd al-Dīn (bracketed), p. 1114.
118 Shīrāzī, p. 51.
119 Shīrāzī, p. 51.
120 Shīrāzī, p. 51.
121 Mustawfī, vol. 2, p. 263.
122 Shīrāzī, p. 52, '*beh ḥājeb birūn raft va az sar karsī dar oftād va wafāt kard*'.

had to go outside for his needs (*beh hājat*), to answer a call of nature, with no mention of croaking ravens or dramatic visions forewarning him of his imminent death which other accounts of his death report. Since his body was showing some signs of life, they carried him back inside the house but he died on the way. He was laid to rest near the bodies of his father and some brothers on the island of Shāhiyeh, today renamed Islamiyeh Island, near the village of Dehkhwārqān.[123] Both Rashīd al-Dīn and Mustawfī express the apprehension felt at Abaqa's demise and both accounts express admiration for the king and the justice of his reign; "When he passed by his crown and throne, fortune turned its face from the Mongols, as a result."[124] Rashīd al-Dīn quotes a contemporary chronogram of his death which begins, "Tyranny became apparent and justice went into obscurity with the death of Abaqa, king of the world."[125] In contrast "Shīrāzī" remains unemotional and non-committal.

Ahmad Tegudar and Arghun Khan

The entries for the years 682/1283 and 683/1284, running to just over 12 edited pages, are concerned with the prolonged conflict between Ahmad and his nephew Arghun Khan. The wealth of dated detail along with the names of the main players, their wives, and associates makes this account an immensely valuable primary source of late thirteenth-century Ilkhanid Iran. What makes this a particularly interesting account is that it can readily be compared and contrasted with other detailed versions of the conflict between these two major figures, in particular the accounts found in Rashīd al-Dīn's *Jāmi' al-Tavārīkh*, Mustawfī's *Zafarnāma*, and even the Safavid chronicler, Khwandamīr's *Ḥabīb al-Siyar*. Again, it is not so much what these accounts share in their reports or how some details differ but more their omissions which are potentially significant. For example, whereas Rashīd al-Dīn and other contemporary sources remark on Ahmad's relationship with the mysterious figure of Īshān Ḥasan Manglī, this disreputable influence is not once mentioned in "Shīrāzī's" account of Ahmad's reign. Shīrāzī's own trip to Egypt as Ahmad's ambassador to the Mamluk court is neither discussed nor even referenced in the *Akhbār-i-Moghūlān*, an omission which perhaps suggests that the author of this chronicle was not Shīrāzī himself.

Ahmad Tegudar is a controversial figure even though his reign was short and regionally uneventful. He was well regarded by Waṣṣāf who described him as "adorned with the necklace of Islam"[126] and abstemious of alcohol,

123 Shīrāzī, p. 52.
124 Mustawfī, vol. 2, p. 264.
125 Rashīd al-Dīn, p. 1118.
126 Waṣṣāf, p. 105, l.23.

"they say the Ilkhan abhorred the drink of the grapevine",[127] but most commentators regard the first claim with doubt and the second as clearly false since Ahmad and his qalandar side-kick, Manglī, spent much of their time incapacitated with hashish and other inebriants. A dispassionate and careful assessment of Ahmad Tegudar's Islamic credentials is provided in Peter Jackson's definitive overview of the region, *The Mongols and the Islamic World,*[128] but for the *Akhbār-i-Moghūlān*, Tegudar's main crime was his fratricidal murder of Qonghurtāī and his faith or lack of it, is not mentioned or even alluded to. Though later chroniclers, commentators, and analysts emphasise the significance of Ahmad's conversion, to his contemporaries the only aspects of his faith that concerned them were the antinomian practices, drink, and drug taking, which clearly interfered with his ability to govern the kingdom. Unacceptable, insulting, and shocking for the noyat, his military elite, was Ahmad's unilateral decision to dispatch Shaykh Abd al-Raḥmān, the Mongol sultan's closest aide, to the Mamluk court to negotiate a peace deal with the Mamluk regime. Such talks would involve negotiating as equals with men, former slaves, whom the Noyat regarded as social, political, tribal, and military inferiors, who had no right to negotiate with a God-appointed sovereign and descendant of Chinggis Khan, the World Conqueror. Not only had Ahmad's act collectively humiliated them, but it was a severe security risk since the Shaykh would have been privy to state secrets and sensitive information, and he had gone to Cairo without the appropriate security. In Cairo, he had been detained, imprisoned, tortured, and interrogated, and, eventually, he was executed or allowed to die and buried while still under Mamluk jurisdiction.

Michael Hope's study of the role of the noyat, the military elite and the Mongol aristocracy around and behind the throne, has thrown new light and a fresh interpretation on the struggles which raged between the lines of all the great chronicles.[129] He elucidates the identity, the role, and the agendas of many of the figures whose names recur without explanation in of all the chronicles, including the *Akhbār*.

One entry recorded by "Shīrāzī" is interesting for what was not said since the incident was of the greatest significance to other actors present at the time. "On Thursday 16th Safar (4th May, 1284), . . . Arghun clashed until sunset with Tubat and Alinaq"[130] at the battle of Āq Khwājeh. Fighting alongside Arghun Khan on this day was the prince's loyal servant, his boon companion

127 Waṣṣāf, 110, l.5.

128 Peter Jackson, *The Mongols and the Islamic World: from Conquest to Conversion*, (New Haven & London: Yale University Press, 2017), pp. 277–279, 347, 362–363.

129 Michael Hope, *Power, Politics, and Tradition in the Mongol Empire and the Īlkhānate of Iran* (Oxford: Oxford University Press, 2016), pp. 138–144.

130 Shīrāzī, p. 57.

or nadīm, ᶜAlā al-Dawlah Simnānī (1261–1336) who came from a well-established family of Persian political administrators, some of whom were solidly entrenched in the Ilkhanid bureaucracy. However, on this particular day, Simnānī who was to achieve great fame as a Sufi poet in later life, underwent a life-changing mystical revelation which so profoundly affected him that when he recovered the next day, he requested that Arghun give him leave to abandon the court and the prince's side so that he could devote his life wholly to God and solely to contemplation. Eventually Arghun granted his friend his wish but not before many attempts and much animated discourse to dissuade him. One of those conversations Simnānī wrote about later, and during their exchange the poet claims, Arghun came close to accepting Islam himself and certainly accepted the concept of One God. With great reluctance Arghun let his friend go and Simnānī held Arghun in the greatest respect for the rest of his life. The episode is of interest when considering the unfounded reputation that Arghun has acquired for being antagonistic to Muslims.[131]

"Shīrāzī's" account presents in chronological order the unfolding events which led from his decision to execute his brother to his own execution as punishment for this act of fratricide. It records the gradual collapse of Ahmad's position as amirs and supporters switched sides, conspired, and abandoned his weakening hold on power. Its importance lies in its detailed naming of the individual players and their interactions with each other. This disruptive phase of the Ilkhanate, which continued after Ahmad's demise in 1284 until Ghazan's assumption of power in 1295, can shed light on the political machinations which rumbled on more beneath the surface during the so-called Golden Age of the Ilkhanate, 1295–1335, a time "admirable and luxuriantly cheerful like the Garden of Paradise, tranquil and secure like the sanctuary of the Ka'ba,"[132] a time which "was the best period of the domination of the Mongols",[133] a time when "the country (was) flourishing and the army well organised [and] the people devoted themselves to joy and pleasure."[134] Azerbaijan is described as a paradise and a common refrain went "It is the time of Bu Saᶜīd, enjoy yourselves; Great God, preserve

131 See Jamal J. Elias, *The Throne Carrier of God: The Life and Thought of ᶜAlā al-Dawlah Simnānī* (Albany: State University of New York Press, 1995), pp. 18–21, for details of this episode and for further citations and references to Semnānī's works. See also George Lane, "Shaykh Chingiz Khan: Maker of the Muslim World", *Journal of Qur'anic Studies*, Vol. 16, No. 1 (2014), pp. 140–155, 143.

132 Maulānā Awliyā' Allāh Āmulī, *Tārīkh-i-Rūyān*, ed. Minūchichr Sutūda (Iran: Intesharat Baniyad va Farsang, 1969/1348), p. 178.

133 Abu Bakr Qoṭbī Aḥārī, *Tārīkh-e Shaykh Ovays*, ed. and tr. J.B. Van Loon (The Hague: Mouton & Co., 1954), Van Loon, p. 51, [facs149]; *Tavārīkh-i-Shaykh Ovays*, ed. Iraj Afshār (Tabriz: Intashārāt Sotudeh, 2010), p. 208/75b [398].

134 Aḥārī, Van Loon, p. 57 [facs 155]; Afshār, p. 214/78b [404].

his Lord!"[135] It should be mentioned, however, that these quotations were written in hindsight, from a period after the collapse of the Ilkhanate when Iran was once again plunged into chaos and anarchy and, thus when considering the earlier period of instability, from 1282–95, the 'Golden Age' 1295–1335, was a period of strong central and monarchical power.

The two final events that are described and scrutinised in this chronicle are firstly, the execution of Ahmad on the night of Thursday 9th August 1284 (25th Jumāda I, 683), after his refusal to answer the charges concerning the murder/execution of his brother, Qonghurtāī, and second, following this, Arghun Khan's coronation on 11th August 1285 (27th Jumāda I, 683). Sultan Ahmad was executed in the same manner that he had killed his own brother, after a *yarghu* court, in both instances, had declared the guilt of the accused party. The edicts of Chinggis Khan laid down that those who damage the "*posht-i-molk*" [back of the country], that is national security, must in turn have their own backs (*posht*) broken.[136] However, Prince Qonghurtāī's fellow defendant, Kuchak Unuqchi, initially escaped the fate of his royal partner in crime and was asked by Ahmad's *yarghu* court to detail the conversations between Qonghurtāī and the royal fugitive, Prince Arghun Khan. Kuchak Unuqchi claimed to have no knowledge of their words and remained silent despite being subjected to 100 strokes of the cane. Ahmad's response to his silence was to declare him "a sly old bastard" (*mardakī pīr gozbuzand*) and to order his execution along with that of his son.[137]

This detailed final section of the chronicle concentrating exclusively on the bitter conflict between the two royal princes, Ahmad and Arghun, poses some intriguing questions and conveniently lends itself to comparison with other Ilkhanid accounts of this divisive dispute. Developments are tracked on an almost daily basis and most of the leading amirs are identified according to their allegiance and the level and nature of their support. It is possible that "Shīrāzī" had realised the fundamental nature of this split that was emerging at the core of the ruling elite, and he understood that the repercussions from this conflict would reverberate long after the death or victory of the leading protagonists. He makes no comment on the role of the Qara'unas army whose troops based in central and western Iran were officially employed in the service of the Ilkhanid state and yet who engaged in operations against Arghun Khan and then later against Ahmad Tegudar while he was officially still the Ilkhan. "Shīrāzī" comments on their violence and plundering but fails to comment on their apparent autonomy. However, it is very revealing that the *Akhbār* reveals how the army of the Qara'unas responds to requests but

135 Aḥārī, Van Loon, p. 57 [facs 155]; Afshār, pp. 214–15/78b [404].

136 Shīrāzī, p. 55.

137 Shīrāzī, p. 55.

never to commands. It emphasises their presence and involvement in this episode far more than Rashīd al-Dīn whose reference stresses their violence, "so thorough that, aside from the ashes in the fireplace, not a trace [of the ordu] remained. [The Qara'unas] left Qutui Khatun, Tödäi Khatun, and Armini Khatun naked, and two thousands of them took up guard over Ahmad."[138]

This edited version of "Shīrāzī's" previously almost unknown chronicle adds to our knowledge of a period of Iranian history which has only recently come under the intense scrutiny of scholars eager to reassess an exciting four decades which, until recently, were idly dismissed as lost to dark barbarian rule. In fact, the creation of the Ilkhanate gave birth to a Persian renaissance and a period of spiritual and cultural regeneration as Iranians looked east and opened their horizons to the potential that was stirring in an emerging Yuan China. These early decades of the Ilkhanate oversaw the blossoming of a Toluid empire where Persian along with Turkish was fast becoming a lingua franca throughout the Eurasian land mass, while individual Persians were assuming power and influence far beyond what would be expected from their numbers. In Iran, also, the glory of the once-reviled Mongol century is being recognised and old texts are not only being re-edited, re-issued, and translated but others, like the *Akhbār* and the *Safīna-ye-Tabrīz*, have been discovered for the first time. In 2002, Ibn Fuwaṭī's history of Baghdad (626–700)[139] was translated into Persian from Arabic, while new editions of Rashīd al-Dīn's lesser known works have regularly appeared over the last decade. Volume I of Shabānkāra'ī's *Majma'-ansāb* was published in 2002, and most exciting of all, the discovery and publication in 2003 of the magnificent literary compendium, the *Safīneh-ye Tabrīzī*,[140] painstakingly copied out by hand by Abu al-Majd, cast the whole culture and literary milieu of Ilkhanid Iran in a new light, revealing Ilkhanid Tabriz to be a far more sophisticated and cultured cosmopolis than previously appreciated. From its opening lines establishing Iran as part of a global, transcultural empire through its chronology underlying the intimacy which existed between Turk and Tajik, this history at least penned by Quṭb al-Dīn Shīrāzī, will prove crucial in establishing a greater understanding of Mongol dominated rule in Iran.

138 Rashīd al-Dīn, p. 1147.

139 In fact, the actual author of this chronicle is unknown and its ascription to Ibn Fuwaṭī is for convenience; Ibn al-Fuwaṭī, *al-Hawādith al-Jāmi'a: Historical events of the 7th Century AH*, translated from the Arabic by ᶜAbdulmuḥammad Āyatī (Tehran: Society for the Appreciation of Cultural Works and Dignitaries, 2002).

140 Abū Majd Muḥammad ibn Masᶜūd Tabrīzī, *Safīneh-ye Tabrīz: A Treasury of Persian Literature and Islamic Philosophy, Mysticism, and Sciences* (Tehran: Iran University Press, 2003).

2 A straight translation

The *Akhbār-i-Moghūlān dar Anbāneh-ye Quṭb*

Akhbār-i-Moghūlān dar Anbāneh-ye Quṭb by Quṭb al-Dīn Shīrāzī, edited by Īraj Afshār, Qum: Grand Library of Āyatollah Mar'ashī Najafī, 2010/1389

Beginning of the Mongol government and the appearance of Chinggis Khan

Bin Yīsūkā bin Qubilā bin Sanqū Bahādar was in the year 599 Hijri, [1202] in the reckoning of the Rumiyans the year 1514, in the reckoning of the Yazdjardi 572, in the Uyghur date, the year of the Pig, and in the Chinese date, the year of the Pig.

Early accounts of Temüjin record events in Wadi Baljuna, which is close to the lands of the Chinese. His followers had gone without food for a few days, when one amongst them succeeded in shooting down a desert sparrow. The bird was cooked and then it was presented to their leader. Temüjin ordered that the bird be divided equally into 70 portions, and from that he took his own share that was no larger than any of the other portions. It was because of his willingness to share the tribulations of his men and because of his righteousness that people became his devotees and followers and were prepared to surrender their souls to him.

From his offspring there were four famous sons who became renowned among the people: Chaghatai Khan, Ögötei Khan, Tolui Khan, and Jochi Khan.

Chaghatai did not live long after his father, and Chinggis Khan appointed Ögötei king in his own lifetime and he placed his son in the position of his own deputy.

He appointed Jochi Khan to the provinces of Qipchaq, Rus, Saqsin, and Bulgar and his descendants ruled there.

The first was Ghūnkarān, after him came Shībān Khan, then Batu Khan, then Berke, then Möngke Temur, and then Tuta Mongke, who is Shah at present, that is in 680/1281–2.

Figure 2.1 Dashi Namdakov's Divine Chinggis

Chinggis assumed semi-divine status amongst his followers as is reflected in this anecdote, biblical in style.

Source: Halcyon Gallery, New Bond St. Reproduced with permission.

After that was the branch of Ögötei Qa'an, who was succeeded by Güyük Khan.

When Güyük died, in consultation with and on the advice of Batu Khan, Möngke Qa'an was enthroned; and the sons of Chaghatai and Ögötei who were not pleased with that decision plotted opposition, and resolved on action against Möngke Khan.

Möngke Khan[1] became aware of their schemes and resolved to meet their machinations with justifiable, considered, and decisive retaliation. Such was the scale of his retaliation with killing, beating, shackling, and the like that not one person from those that had been accomplices in insubordination was exempted, though not one innocent person suffered loss.

The like of the justice and equity in the time of Möngke Khan had seldom existed before. During his time the wolf and the sheep would drink water together.

[21]

When Möngke Khan had resolved the affairs of that vast empire, consisting of the provinces of Turkestan, northern China, Transoxiana, Tibet, and Tangut, he sent his own brother Hülegü to sort out the lands beyond the Oxus, namely the provinces of the Arabs and the Persians.

[22] year 650 odd/1252

Hülegü Khan came in the year six hundred and fifty-odd to subdue the land from Khorasan until he reached Damascus; and he took all of Khorasan, Jabāl, Kirman, and Ghaznīn until Multan, and much of the country of Hind, and Iraq-i-'Ajam and Iraq-i-'Arab, as well as Mazanderan, and the lands from Arran, Shirwan, and Darband as far as the interior of the Qipchaq steppe. He brought an army from Rus, and with that army plundered the deserts of Arabia. And before [accomplishing all] this, he had [already] seized the caliph of Baghdad himself and taken all the sultans of Diyarbakir and Syria.

And Hülegü became the ruler in Rum and the [land of] the Franks [Palestine]. These lands, which – if anyone heard tell of them, they would be astonished – were open to him in total, that is, from Transoxiana to Damascus, from the deserts of Iraq-i 'Arab to Russia, and from Hind to Khwarazm. We had seen Hülegü in his court enough times to see that in one day he dealt efficiently with the affairs of this province [presumably Azerbaijan] and that in every one of the provinces under his command, he governed well, in such a way that his justice was total wherever was *īl* to him.

When Hülegü had passed over the River Oxus, he arrived in Khorasan. After that he assembled around himself many armies from Turkestan, northern China [Khiṭā], and Transoxiana with men and armaments beyond count, such as the '*Kamān-hā-ye cherkh*,' a crossbow that drew three bows with one string.

1 No explanation is offered for the switch from using Qa'an to Khan.

[23]

[Every] Three bows fired one arrow and each of their arrows was nearly three-quarters of a *gaz* [approx. metre] in length including the point. The shaft of the point came up to the notch of the arrow and the feather extended from the notch to the point, such that they had attached the feather of a vulture or an eagle to the shaft of the arrow.

All arrows were turned, not shaved, with a plane or a knife, and the mangonel arrows were made from white poplar wood and enclosed in the skin

Figure 2.2 Crossbow, Ulun Baatar Airport

One of these wooden crossbows could well have been transported to Iran as described in the *Akhbār-ye-Moghūlān*.

Photo by author

of horse and cow rind in the same way as the scabbard of a knife or sword is covered. Of these mangonel arrows, on every mangonel five or seven are tied together and set with putty.

All these machines were brought from Turkestan on vehicles with skilled and competent operatives. And from that locality, namely the border of Khorasan, Hülegü Khan ordered decrees to be written and messengers dispatched to the rulers and kings of the provinces, saying: "I am setting out against the Heretics.[2] If you send assistance in the form of troops and armaments, provisions and military supplies, I will count it as a favour and your province will have peace and security. But if you neglect to do this, as soon as I become free from my present concerns, I will deal with you and after that no excuses or apology will be acceptable."

[24]

So, in response, they came: kings like the Atābek of Fārs Muẓaffer al-Dīn Abū Bakr bin Saᶜd and the sultans of Rum 'Izz al-Dīn and Rukn al-Dīn; as well as the rulers of Khorasan, Sistan, Mazanderan, Kirman, Rustamdār, Sherwān, Georgia, Iraq, Azerbaijan, Arran, Lurestan, and more, some accompanied by their own people.

The remainder, who did not come in person, sent brothers and relatives with armies, provisions, supplies, ceremony, servants, and their allegiance and gifts to serve their new king.

From all the provinces, Hülegü's commanders arranged the distribution of provisions and supplies without limit and beyond compare transported by donkey, camel, cow, asses ["long ears"], and such like. Such was the organisation that noodles, cooked porridge, and pounded millet had been brought from the provinces of Northern China and Uyghuristan to the foot of Alamut and Mīmūndaz and that castle, Girdkūh; and every half *farsang* they had stacked so much flour, rice, and necessities (staples) in bags of fine linen [that] everywhere great hills appeared.

[25] year 651–1253/4

From Khorasan, Hülegü sent his massed armies to Qohestan. First, in Rabīᶜ al-Aval of the year 651/May 1253, he sent an army to the foot of Girdkūh and he overcame the fortifications, the like of which no one has ever seen.

2 "Shīrāzī" does not use this term himself, here putting it in the mouth of Hulegu. He uses the term Ismā'īliyān.

They dug a huge moat surrounding the castle, and behind the moat they built a fortified wall, and after the wall they built sheltered houses, and after the houses they built another wall and another moat after that. In this way, if anyone from inside the castle attempted to break out, or if anyone from outside planned to break in, in order to relieve the people within the castle, the moats and the fortified walls would act as a deterrent from both directions.

Hülegü Khan himself went to the foot of the castle and for one or two days conducted the battle. Because these measures against the defenders of the castle were not proving easy, he assigned the entire army to that place and the grandest commanders were appointed to this campaign.

[26]

And after approximately one year, cholera struck and a great many of the people of the castle died. The news was taken to ᶜAlā' al-Dīn Moḥammad, pādeshāh of the Ismā'īlīs, informing him that not one man remained in the castle of Girdkūh and it would invariably be lost. 'Alā' al-Dīn sent 100 men under the army commander, Moqdam al-Dīn Moḥammad Mobāraz in order to break through the cordon and allow his squadron to pass through that body of men that were besieging the castle. None of that company of men apart from one man who fell into the moat and broke his leg but who was safely removed, was injured.

And those 100 men reached the castle and they were able to work at strengthening the fortifications and for nearly 20 years that castle remained besieged. However, finally, when the defenders surrendered, all of them were killed.

[27] year 653/1255

In Zū al-Q'adeh of the year 653/ Dec 1255, an apostate who had become a special retainer of the Khwarshāh, and on whom he relied, killed ᶜAlā' al-Dīn Moḥammad.

His son, Rukn al-Dīn Ḥasan, whom they called Khwarshāh, took the throne in place of his father. Rukn al-Dīn Ḥasan sent a brother named Shāhanshāh to the presence of Hülegü so that he could declare that: "though my father was not *īl* (loyal, subservient), I am *īl* and willing to serve you."

This Shāhanshāh went to Nishapur and arrived to present himself before Hülegü. He was seized and taken to Iraq.

Rukn al-Dīn sent another prince who would offer homage. "Let him [Hülegü] send my brother back from the province of Ray so that he can appear before us again." Though the brother had left with 200 men, he was returned with only ten persons and a terse command, "Go ! If Rukn al-Dīn cannot come himself, he should send us another brother or son."

[28]

On the advice of his wazir, [Khwāja Aṣīl al-Dīn Zozanī], Rukn al-Dīn sent another brother named Shīrānshāh with a number of rare gifts. But when Hülegü said, "Since you have become *īl*, be secure", the conqueror was thinking, "they are unaware that our army has appeared in their province." When the Ismā'īlīs sent a representative to speak with those Mongol amirs asking "We have become *īl*, why then have you come to our lands?" Those amirs answered "since a state of submission (*īlī*) and concord now exists, we have come to graze our horses."

As soon as Hülegü reached the border of their province, he fell upon them with thundering hooves. If it had not been for the excessive rainfall that night, it is possible that they would have captured Rukn al-Dīn at the foot of the castle.

However, Rukn al-Dīn, realising the danger of his situation, returned to the castle at daybreak.

In one hour, armies arrived from every direction, surrounding the castle in numbers no one until that time had ever seen. They could not believe that such numbers of men as they witnessed were possible to muster, for Hülegü's armies had so occupied mountain, thicket and plain that in no direction was there a path for a single foot-soldier. In less than a night and day all around the castle that rose like a mighty mountain, the besieging army had formed a *nerge* that encircled the castle for a distance of approximately six *farsangs*.

After 13 days, with the approval and consultation of the nobles and ministers of his government, Rukn al-Dīn emerged from his castle and went to prostrate himself before Hülegü. When Hülegü saw him, he realised that he was a child and lacked experience and guile. He reassured the Khwarshāh with sweet words, and sent someone to evacuate all the castellans and people from all the forts that they possessed in Khorasan, Qumis, Rudbar, and Syria. The result was that they surrendered all the castles, which numbered more than a hundred, apart from Girdkūh, which has itself been mentioned and which remained under siege for about 20 years, and the fortress of Lamasar, in which there were relatives of Rukn al-Dīn and which they preserved for more than a year. Though the people of that fortress perished of pestilence and sickness, nobody emerged from any of the other castles, which were more than 100, with even a nose bleed.

Finally, he sent Rukn al-Dīn to see Möngke Qa'an.

[29]

When they brought him to a place where he was allowed to be by himself, it was there that he was killed. Between Qazvin and Abhar, the remaining brothers, his children, the women of his harem, and his dependents were killed and that [Ismā'īlī] state ceased to exist.

[30] year 655/1257

From that place, at the beginning of the year 655/1257, Hülegü busied himself with the group of kings and the people of the Jibāl, as for example in Tang, Kulīn, and Īveh and such places, and carried them off.

In Shawāl 655/ October 1257, he mounted his horse and set off from Hamadan for Baghdad, which he reached in three months. Every day he travelled no more than two *farsang*s. He organised his armies in such a way that from the province of Fars until the province of Rum, one body of men without limit and number descended upon Baghdad.

The army of Fars and Kirman came by way of Khuzestan and Shushtar. It was such that the army's left wing came by the shores of the Sea of Oman and the right wing had merged with their troops from Iraq and the rest. The army of Rum proceeded from the border of Syria and Diyarbakr in such a way that their left wing joined with the armies of Arran and Azerbaijan while at the same time they poured from all sides into Iraq-i-'Arab. The first party to reach Baghdad and confront the army of Baghdad was commanded by Prince Buqa Temur, Baiju Noyan, and Suqunjaq Noyan. They say *noyan* for *amir* in the Mongol language.

[31]

Each one of these amirs had ten or 15 thousand men. In Baghdad they reached the Jarīt. The Caliph's army, whose leader and commander was Mujāhad al-Dīn Bebakaraz Dawātdār, whom they called the Lesser Dawātdār, who was the axis of the army and the government of the caliph Musta'ṣim bil'allah Abū Aḥmad, went to confront the enemy army and their vanguard, which comprised four or five thousand men and which was commanded by Suqunjaq Noyan. The Dawātdār's army struck the Mongol forces and completely routed them and forced them to retreat four *farsangs* from the regions of Dajīl to Bashīriyeh, and when night came Suqunjaq's forces remained in that very same place and the army of Baghdad did not enter the town.

For two nights Suqunjaq maintained contact with that army that Buqa Temur and Baiju commanded, while they meanwhile made their way to join Suqunjaq. They sent their own armies to surround the [Caliph's] armies of

Baghdad, and as dawn broke, they raised a shout and put hands to sword. They say that the army of Baghdad was drowned in the sea.

The Dawātdār with a troop of horsemen fell upon the invaders and escaped [back to Baghdad] while a group of famished Turks who had broken out in a different direction escaped in the direction of Syria.

Hülegü approached from the direction of the Khorasan Road, and from the Dawātdār's army the slain were retrieved and from them 12,000 ears were severed. These ears were sent to Hülegü, but this total excluded the ears of those who had fled from the battlefield and had then fallen into the water and streams.

[32]

When Hülegü reached Baghdad the rest of his army, who were already in the city, was standing on the ramparts. Because a great assemblage of people, namely all the people of the Sawād, had come to the city before the Mongol army arrived, there was a great dearth, want, and scarcity of provisions in Baghdad. Pestilence struck and many people died. The number of deaths reached the point that the Ministry's priority was to prepare the corpses and bury them. Meanwhile the situation deteriorated so much that the people of Baghdad could no longer cope with ablutions and burial of the dead, so bodies were thrown into the Tigris. In the end, it became so bad that they could not even carry the dead to the Tigris on account of the number who were dying, as the porters did not have time and were no longer turning up. At this point the caliph commanded that an empty property be assigned for each area and the dead be put there and as it filled and as they found the opportunity, they would bury them. Even when the army arrived, they were unable to cope with the situation.

Hülegü reached the city of Baghdad and ordered the erection of mangonels. He set up a single tower carrying 16 mangonels at the Aleppo Gate and the Gate of Triumph. They hurled rocks of 100 to 5 *mann* and during one day and night they pulverised the stronghold that they called the Persian Tower.

Because mangonel stone could not be found in the vicinity of Baghdad, they brought rocks from Jelūlā and Jabal al-Ḥamrīn. They cut up palm trees with handsaws and hurled them with the mangonel.

When the people grew afraid, the caliph sought quarter and announced, "We will make peace and we will surrender."

[33]

Hülegü commanded that the Mongols that had gone to the top of the battlements should not descend. "They must remain there until they [the caliph's advisers] emerge!" He sent a message saying, "If you are *īl* send out the army so that we can count them and in due course we can seek out people who may be useful to us." The caliph ordered that his army should go outside to surrender and Hülegü sent a *yarliq* and *paiza* for the commanders of the caliph's army, first the Dawātdār and afterwards Sulīmānshāh and the rest, saying, "Let them come forth and bring their troops, so that when I go to Syria they may provide assistance".

When the army of Baghdad resolved to come out, countless people from those who were not military or army also came out. They supposed that in so far as they came forth they might find safety, and it would be worse in the city. In fact, the opposite was true, for those in the city who remained hidden in holes, furnaces, and dark places remained safe and unharmed while those who came outside were divided up and distributed into 10,000s, 1000s, 100, and 10s and they were all killed. It was thus since Hülegü had commanded that they be counted and 1,022,000 humans were slain.

They brought out the caliph after Hülegü had entered the city and feasted in his palace. Hülegü's court decamped from the city to a village that they call Waqaf. Then they came outside the city.

[34] events of the year 656/1258

[On the] day . . . [at the time of the] afternoon prayer . . .[3] in the year 656/1258 they martyred the caliph, and they martyred his two eldest sons – whether before or after him, is not known – and the armies returned from there. The weather had become warm and the great stench penetrated the brains of the people.

Pestilence struck and most of the Mongol army became sick, and many died of the disease. They came to the provinces of Sīāh Kūh and Hamadan.

Hülegü became sick for 20 days and then he became well.

He went to Arran and Mūqān for the winter, and at the end of the winter he sent the army with his son Yoshmūt to Diyarbakir. They went and lay siege to Mayyāfāriqīn. Yoshmūt returned at the beginning of summer.

[35] year 657 (1258/59)

In the spring of this year, that is the year 657/1258, Hülegü went himself to Syria and conquered all the country of Diyarbakir and Syria. They killed

3 There is a blank space in these two positions on the original ms.

the greater number of the people of Aleppo; and the people of Damascus sent messengers and gifts, and Sultan Malek Nāsir had left to avoid war. The Sultan had gone in the direction of Egypt and Yemen.

Hülegü had sent a *shahneh*[4] and governor to Damascus, 'Alā' al-Dīn Jāstī (Hashi) and Qāḍī Shams al-Dīn Qomī. It was surprising that many of the people of Damascus were generally Yazīdī (derogatory term for Sunni)[5] and each of these were Qomī Shi'ites.[6] The people of Damascus were so happy with them that not for one moment did any affliction disturb these two great ones.

[36] year 658 (1259–60)

In the year 658/1259–60 there were few amirs in rank and status greater than Ket Buqa Noyan, around whom the Mongol army revolved, and there was no one greater in manliness or judgement, and after him victory nowhere never again fell to the Mongol army.

He was in Ba'lbek in the summer with one tūmān [10,000 soldiers] of the Mongol army. The troops of Syria and Egypt were all under the Sultanate of Quduz, sultan through his sedition against the Kāmiliyān[7] who had been sultans of Syria and Egypt. They came to be of one language, and assembled in Kerak and Shawbak.[8]

Ket Buqa had given Baidar, who was an amir, his own advance guard and had sent him to the Gaza plain.

As Quduz moved on Syria, Baidar sent a message to Ket Buqa saying "Our army is ready, what is your command?"

4 A *Shahneh* in Persian, a *Basqaq* in Turkish and a *Daraghuchi* in Mongolian, and roughly interchangeable terms meaning an overseer or representative of the imperial power, appointed by the Khan to whom he would report back and whose interests he would protect.

5 Yazīd ibn Mu'āwiya ibn Abī Sufyān, 20 July 647–11 November 683, second Umayad Caliph who had Husain killed at the battle of Kerbala, October 10, 680/ 10 Muharram, 61.

6 Qom is an Iranian holy city, 125 kms south-west of Tehran, which houses the shrine of Fatima al-Mu'sumeh, sister of Ali, Imam Reza (d.818).

7 Ayyubids 1171–1260; al-Malik al-Kamil Naser ad-Din Abu al-Ma'ali Muhammad) (c. 1177–1238) the fourth Kurdish Ayyubid sultan of Egypt. Under sultan Kamīl [Meledin], the Ayyubids defeated the Fifth Crusade but as a result of the Sixth Crusade, he ceded Jerusalem to the Franks and is known to have met with Saint Francis.

8 These were the Mamluks of Cairo who challenged the Ilkhans originally for regional hegemony and later for the leadership of the Islamic world. The Mamluks harboured a claimant to the Abbasid Caliphate. They were ethnic Turks, Qipchaqs-Cumans, Caucasians, Circassians, and even Turco-Mongols sold or captured as slave soldiers.

Figure 2.3 Mongol Horses, Inner Mongolia

Mongol horses are surprisingly small, more like ponies and yet it was their horses which enabled the Chinggisid archers to conquer the world.

Photo by author

[37]

Ket Buqa cautioned not to take another step back until he himself arrived. By the time the reply reached Baidar, the army of Quduz was upon him and they put him to flight. Ket Buqa arrived and cruelly demanded of him, "Why didn't you stand your ground until you were killed in that same place?" Baidar replied, "I couldn't stand, would you have?"

The next day before dawn the Syrian army came upon Ket Buqa,[9] and not a horse's head turned. Anyone from the army of Ket Buqa who did not flee was killed in that very same place; and Quduz's men chased the remainder from the province of Gaza to the city of Homs and the shores of the river Orontes. Ket Buqa was killed in the same place that he was captured. The Syrian and Egyptian army also captured Ket Buqa's sons and wives and other women and boys of his army that were in Ba'lbek and other places in Syria.

Also, in the middle of these altercations and the war, following the instigation and consultation of Rukn al-Dīn Bekodesh Bunduqdār, Quduz Sultan himself was assassinated, along with his retainers and relatives.

Rukn al-Dīn Bekodesh Bunduqdār [Baybars, 1223–1 July 1277] was enthroned as sultan of Egypt and Syria, and with imperial pomp he assumed

9 This was the battle of Ayn Jalūt in Palestine where the Mongols suffered their 'first' major defeat. It had symbolic rather than military significance.

control of that country. Never before had history witnessed a person that had such judgement and foresight. His first commands were the prohibition of wine, and for notables, military officers, and Turks, the prohibition of assembly and deliberation, and the seizure of all of the cities on the shore of the Foreign Sea from Alexandria as far as the province of Sīs [ancient capital of Cilician Armenia, south-west of Kozan in Adana Province].

On one occasion, 700 Franks conspired to commit acts of deceit on their Muslim neighbours. They claimed that in a dream their hearts had become so fearful of their Frankish religion and faith that they had become Muslims. "We have come to serve the sultan so that after the religion of Islam has been presented and taught to us, we will be given a place in a school so that we can learn the Qur'an and we will become expert in the Sunna of Islam and the Shariah."

[38]

They had planned that when Bunduqdār trusted them, on the day of the festival when Muslims come out and the people of Islam stand together in prayer, they would put hand to sword and strike out against the Muslims.

God Almighty wished that Bunduqdār be aware of this situation. Bunduqdār commanded that the Franks be treated well and until the day of the 'Īd, he entrusted them to the care of a group of men. The Franks' designs were given away as two men took each of them by the shoulders. Bunduqdār's men realised that under their clothes all of them were wearing a coat of mail and a kaftan and underneath this they had short swords of Damascus steel which were seized. Thus, the Franks were bound and carried to the place of the 'Īd celebration, and there they were held.

Bunduqdār commanded his men to address the Franks thus, "First you must learn to stand in prayer. Afterwards we will instruct you in the sacrifice." When the Muslim community had performed their prayers Bunduqdār ordered that they be cast in the manner of the sacrificial animal and their necks were slit with a knife in the same way as in the rites of the sacrifice.

When their clothes were removed, all of them were wearing fine coats of mail and fine kaftans. As soon as word of their finery reached the common people, they stripped them naked and from that time fear and dread that defies description entered into the hearts of the Franks and the Rūmiyeh. The few times that Hulegu sent an army to Syria, they [the Franks and the Rūmiyeh] would do nothing.

[39]

After that, enmity arose between Hülegü and his kinsmen, and on account of their hostility Hülegü did not set out for Syria or Egypt but instead fought with Berke. A few times Hülegü went as far as Berke's lands,[10] in such a way that he passed a few *farsangs* beyond the gateway [*Darband*][11] to Saqsīn[12] and crossed the Terek River.[13] Finally, feeling secure, Hülegü's army struck camp among the houses and chattel that belonged to Berke's army based in the province of Qipchaq. Berke's forces gathered from all directions and charged down upon Hülegü's forces.

This army had become negligent and had allowed great calamity to fall upon them and in a rout, they came unto the seaport of Shābarān[14] [in Shirvan]. A great number of Hülegü's soldiers met death and destruction and Hülegü suffered greatly from this episode. He debated what kind of retaliation and retribution he might take for this affair, but he was incapacitated by black thoughts, and however much he tried to compose himself he relapsed into those dark thoughts once more.

At this time also, Hülegü had elevated the son of the Lesser Dawātdār,[15] who they called Jalāl al-Dīn, to a grand position, and the khan imagined to himself that there was nobody dearer or more trustworthy in the whole of his territories or army.

This Jalāl declared that there were still a few thousand Qipchaq Turks in the caliph's territories that knew the roads and understood the customs of that province [the Caucasus region]. If the king commanded, he would go and summon them so that "when you command us to return to the war against Berke, we may take them so that they may go ahead and provide us with intelligence."

[40]

Forasmuch as Hülegü prior to this had seized Berke's soldiers and the persons who belonged to that quarter, and had killed some and imprisoned some, while others had fled, the grounds for this episode, the outbreak of hostilities with Berke, had become manifest in the year that Baghdad was taken [656/1258], when Balghāī, Tūtār, and Tūlī, who were Berke's close

10 According to the *Yuan Si*, Mongke had allotted Georgia to Berke.

11 Means gateway and also the city, Darband was in fact a port on the Caspian which traditionally held back the hellish forces of Gog and Magog, which also acted as a border between the Jochid Khanate and the Ilkhanate.

12 The location of Saqsīn is much debated. It was a mediaeval city that flourished from the eleventh to the thirteenth centuries. It was situated in the Volga Delta, or in the Lower Volga region, and was known in pre-Mongol times as Saksin-Bolgar, which in Mongol times became Sarai Batu.

13 Rises in the Caucasus in N. Georgia, flows north through Ossetia and Chechnya, then drains into the Caspian in Daghestan.

14 Situated on the coast of modern-day north Azerbaijan.

15 Caliph's chamberlain, Aybak.

kinsmen, indeed his nephews, exercised authority in the realm. If ever Hülegü nominated their forces for some task, they would openly say, "Since our troops do most of the work, let him, namely Hülegü, not threaten us." They harboured sentiments of this kind and from time to time they would pass remarks. Factious persons exaggerated the situation and reported things to the king, and for this reason he grew angry with them. It was also the case that Berke's *shaḥna*s and governors and his family held the choicest and best territories in Khorasan, Iraq, Azerbaijan, Arrān, and Georgia, and used to say, "These are our royal lands", which means, their private property. And on every possible occasion factious persons would say things to aggravate the situation.

[41] events from the year 656/1256 **[these events appear to break the chronological order]**

Around that juncture, in the year 656/1258, Balghāī died in the course of a feast [*ṭūy*]. After a short interval, Tūtār in turn was accused of sorcery and was sent to Berke for having done such a thing. Berke declared, "Since he is guilty, let Hülegü arrange it". Tūtār was brought back and Hülegü gave orders for his execution. This became the grounds for hostilities, so some years later Hülegü sent this Jalāl, the Dawātdār's son, to Baghdad for the reason that has previously been described, to bring back troops. The Ilkhan issued Jalāl al-Dīn with an edict: "Anyone from whom this Jalāl should deem prudent to ask, should furnish all horses, weapons, harnesses, provisions and funds; neither the governors of Baghdad nor any other living being should interfere in his activities, until he has accomplished what we have decreed."

[42] year 662/1263

Jalāl went to Baghdad in the year 662/1263 and everybody recognised him. Those that spoke with him said that this is a man who is ready whether in the military or in other kinds of work. Jalāl al-Dīn sought them out and in secret said "The king has sent me to lead you into battle so that you can serve him in the front lines of the army. His intention is that you will die there, on the frontline, or you will make your name famous. If you are killed in that place, in your stead there are others who will continue the very same work."

"Now you all know me and whose son I am. I will not allow you to become sword fodder in the cause of an infidel. Although the king remains extremely favourable towards me, my intention is that we declare our abandonment of this infidel state and fate. I will cast off the hand of these Mongols from myself and you."

[43]

When he had spoken these words, all were beguiled by his promises and an army was assembled. He immediately mounted before his troops and beat the drums and passed over the bridge to Baghdad to attack the Khafājeh Arabs, plundering a few oxen and camels. Jalāl al-Dīn took horses, weapons, pay, and complete provisions from Baghdad's treasury for the numbers of troops he had collected, and ordered that muster to decamp with their women, children, and everything else they possessed and again he beat the drum before crossing over the bridge.

He said, "Let us take our women and children along with us to visit the holy shrines of the Imams, since after this my residence will be the province of Darband and those regions, and we will not have chance to return here. We men will go and take provisions, that is, plunder, for the road from the Khafājeh Arabs." And he went.

When he had crossed the Euphrates, Jalāl al-Dīn said to his own wives and the ordinary soldiers, "I have the idea of going to Syria and Egypt. Everyone who agrees, well and good, wonderful but otherwise those who so wish must turn back now from here." Even if in their hearts they did not want to go, they could not bring themselves, from fear, to say that they would return and so immediately adopting the manner of the enthusiast and the occupied they set out for Syria.

When this news reached the king's ears his anger was beyond description. For a long time, Hülegü wrung his hands, ground his teeth, and moaned that a little one should not tease him like this and such deceit was in excess of anything. He suffered a relapse of his ailments and sickness overcame him. He was seized by epilepsy and of all the kinds of doctors who attended him none were able to cope, for they did not know a cure.

[44] year 663 (1264/65)

In Rabī' al-Akhar in the year 663/January 1265, on the border of Maragheh on the banks of the river that they call the Jaghātū, Hülegü passed away. He had 13 sons.

Meanwhile, his oldest son, Abaqa, was in Khorasan and Yoshmut was on the border of Shirwan and Darband, so someone was sent to summon them. Neither arrived while Hülegü lived.

Yoshmut arrived on the third day after his father's death and he resided at court two days for consultation concerning official affairs and then returned to his own place.

Abaqa arrived after a few days from the province of Sitārbāḍ and Gorgān and he also did not stay in Hülegü's ordu, returning early to his own place.

Dokuz Khatun, who had been the wife of Tolui Khan, also died in that week. She had enjoyed great authority and her orders were always executed.

After a short time, five or six months later, they convened a quriltai [*qūrīltāī*][16] and Abaqa was placed on the throne.

[45] The following paragraph is almost incomprehensible in the original manuscript:

> He cared greatly for the troops . . . a period of 17 years . . . these regions that have been mentioned and his father had captured . . . machination repeatedly? . . . in such a way that he did no harm to . . . that in ruins . . . they did, they took, and they killed and in . . . before they came . . . done sufficiently . . . they were with the Mongol and great and difficult work that he . . . because Hülegü's war . . . he with Mongol when Berke . . . that with difficult . . .

[46] year 667/1258–59

In the year 667, the senior wife of Hülegü, Qutui Khatun, because of the disorder in that province, arrived from Turkestan. Her two elder sons, Takeshī[n][17] and Tekūdār (later Sultan Ahmad), who had wives and children, accompanied her.

Abaqa had great respect for them and gave them a great many possessions and land. His own concubine named Ārqān was from the house of Qutui Khatun. She had come with Hülegü from that place, from Qutui's ordu, and whatever was Qutui Khatun's share, this Ārqān used to appropriate it. At the time of the death of Hülegü, she struck herself with a knife and killed herself. When Qūtī Khatun came to her home, it so happened that her house was richly decorated with a variety of items.

Abaqa arrived from the province of Diyarbakr and Miyāfārqīn and he awarded Qutui Khatun a few provinces, from which each year she accrued about 100,000 *Khalīftī* dinar, and that income was squandered foolishly.

Even though Abaqa would continually lavish them with gifts, attention, provisions, flocks, and herds, they [Qutui's party] resented his position as sovereign.

[47]

A short while later Yoshmut, whose summer domicile was in Georgia, and in winter resided at the confines of Ganjeh and Bardaᶜa, died. After him, Tekshī[n] died.

16 Convocation, jamboree, council meeting of Mongol elite to decide on matters of state.
17 This should be Takshin; Prince Takshī was the son of Böchök, half-brother of Hulegu.

Yoshmut had a brother, a very brave and judicious man who used to represent Abaqa in Khorasan. He also died.

Abaqa Khan allowed every country and region that he had given to his brothers to pass on to their offspring and he made no difficulty for any of them.

[48] year 675 (1276/77)

In the year 675, Bunduqdār of Syria took an army to Rum; and in that place, there were two great amirs with a great army. These special Mongols were called Tūqū bin Elkāī and Tūdavān bin Sodūn.[18]

Rukn al-Dīn Bunduqdār (d. 1277) engaged them in battle in Ābolestān of Rum. He destroyed that army, killed those two amirs, and took up his residence for a short time at Caesarea in Rum, in anticipation of what Mo^{c}īn al-Dīn Parvana,[19] who was lord of Rum, had perchance promised him. "If you come, I will give you the crown of Rum." The Parvāna feared that the Mongols would act treacherously towards him.

Because Rukn al-Dīn Bunduqdār remained in Caesarea for close to a week and he did not allow or give permission for his own army to plunder, sustaining that army became difficult. The Parvāna did not present himself before him and had retreated to a castle and remained there. Bunduqdār withdrew from Rum towards Syria.

When news reached Abaqa, he set out in person for Rum with a vast army. But by the time he was on the move, Bunduqdār had gone, so Abaqa returned.

[49]

The next year Abaqa set out for Syria. He himself went to Raḥbeh in Syria, and he sent his brother Möngke Temur (1256–82), the son of Uljayi Khatun, to whom he had given command of the army, to Syria by way of Diyarbakir.

18 These were Elgäi Noyan's son and Suqunjaq Noyan's brother.

19 Mu'īn al-Dīn Sulaiman Parvāna, r.1261–77; In 1277, Baybars entered the Seljuk sultanate and on 18 March, overcame the Mongol army in Elbistan, while the Pervāneh, who was in command of the Saljuq forces expected by both Baybars and the Mongols, took flight to Tokat along with the young sultan. Baybars made a triumphal entry into Kayseri on 23 April and then returned to Syria. At the news of his troops' defeat, Abaqa hastened to Anatolia (July 1277) and punished the Saljuqi Turks, sources citing massacres of tens of thousands of people. Deeming him responsible for Baybars's foray into Anatolia, Abaqa also had Pervāneh killed, eaten according to Hetoum, on 2 August 1277.

Möngke Temur[20] set off and he confronted a Syrian army on the borders of Homs and Hama. By this time, Bunduqdār had died, and the king and commander of that country was called Alfī,[21] a Qipchaq Turk who had also been a slave of the sultans of Syria, namely the family of Salāh al-Dīn. They battled, and the army of Prince Möngke Temur was severely routed and forced to retreat.

Abaqa Khan was extremely pained from this outcome and he would not turn his face to his brother. He said that it was clear that the following year he would go himself to see what could be done. He spent the winter in Baghdad.

They [had] seized 'Alā' al-Dīn, the Ṣāḥib Dīvān, and mulcted him, plundering all his palaces and houses and placing a double yoke on his neck. The foundation for this calamity had been laid one year previously by Majd al-Mulk Yazdī. He had thrust himself into Abaqa's service, after 40 or 50 persons, all scribes and men of distinction, had come forward to attack and harass the ṣāḥib-dīwāns, 'Alā' al-Dīn Aṭā Malik and Shams al-Dīn Muḥammad; and there were many grandees of whom the people calculated that they would one day work for the dismissal of the ṣāḥibs. However, not a soul suspected that behind such an affair lay a hand like that of Majd al-Mulk [Yazdī].

[50] year 679/1280–81

Meanwhile Majd al-Mulk in the season of spring of the year 679/1281 in Sharūyāz, in between Abhar and Zangān at the Muslim Fort, presented himself before Abaqa in the hot baths of the slaughterhouse and explained this matter to him. Prior to this situation arising, Abaqa had grown estranged from the [Juwaynī] brothers and sought a pretext to act against them.

When Majd al-Mulk spoke about the state of the court finances, they [the Juwaynīs] became afraid and very uncomfortable. But Shams al-Dīn bore up as had been his custom in the past and he was not made to appear.

'Alā' al-Dīn was summoned from Baghdad, and when he arrived in Siah Kuh[22] they demanded that the property of his that he had taken from the king must be returned. Majd al-Dīn ibn Athīr presided in front of him probing whether he had acquired the property from this or that person or place.

20 Youngest brother of Abaqa; he married Abish Khatun of Shiraz.

21 Al-Malik al-Manṣūr Saif ad-Dīn Qalāʾūn al-Alfi as-Ṣālihī an-Najmī al-ʿAlāʾī, r.1279–90; sold for 1000 dinars in 1240s into household of Sultan al-Kamīl.

22 This had been the site of Abaqa's summer pastures. It was a mountain overlooking the town of Kalandar in Azerbaijan, near the source of the Jaghatu River.

Shams al-Dīn had told his brother not to renounce his principles unless they torture him and reminded him that wealth is not worth lost honour. 'Alā' al-Dīn was put in a headlock so that he would surrender 300 tūmān of gold to them.

[51]

When they returned to Maragheh from Siah Kuh, Abaqa, with all of his amirs and the pillars of the government and many of the royal ladies, was in the Butkhāneh [*Buddhist temple*].

That day Abaqa commanded that they write a royal proclamation on behalf of Majd al-Mulk to be read before the assembled people. Everyone was in agreement that Mongol kings had never before granted anyone such a *yarlīgh*.

When they proclaimed the *yarlīgh*, Abaqa told Majd al-Mulk that he must pay great attention to affairs of state, the administration, the treasury, and the livestock and all that is his. "Watch closely everything your deputies do and keep guard on yourself and never be separated from me. Anyone who is an enemy to you is an enemy to me. Those that are friends with you are friends of mine. Henceforth, if anyone makes an attack on you, I will be with you."

Because Abaqa had issued such an extreme mark of favour, the whole network of amirs and notables was disrupted, and Majd al-Mulk sent deputies to all the notables, all the tax districts and provinces, everywhere from within Rum to the end of Khorasan and from the deserts of Arabia until the borders of Saqsīn.[23] He raised an edifice the likes of which nobody had ever seen. In the space of seven or eight months a person who had been of no account anywhere now managed a business of such great complexity. Everybody was amazed.

When they returned from Maragheh to Baghdad, as has been mentioned, they confiscated lands from the minister ᶜAlā' al-Dīn.

[52] year 680 [1281/82]

At the end of winter Abaqa went to Hamadan. He had a very great love of wine and he would drink excessively. He drank in Bahrāmshāh's house[24] until night; and in the middle of the night, he had a need to go outside, and from on top of the lavatory he fell off and died. It was such that a little life remained in his body so they carried him into the house. He died on the way.

23 Volga delta, with the capital in Sarai Batu.
24 This reference remains obscure.

This was on 20th Ḍu al-Ḥijja 680 (1st April 1282). Abaqa's body was taken to the burial site of his father and of some of his brothers, on the island that is known as Shahiyeh in the centre of Azerbaijan near Dehkhwārqān.

[53]

In consultation with all of the princes, that is Abaqa's brothers and his sons, they seated Prince Tegüdar, whom they call Sultan Ahmad, on the royal throne on 26th Moharram 681 (6th May 1282).

[54] year 682 (1283/84)

In the year 682/1283–84 Sultan Ahmad sent his brother, known as Qonghartai, to rule Rum. The Sultan appointed Qonghartai the commander of the army which accompanied him to Anatolia (Rum). This army enabled him to deal with the rebels and to protect Rum from the Syrian army.

Qonghartai arrived in Rum with his army and behaved mercilessly towards people who were very loyal (*īl*), cooperative, and contributive, massacring and enslaving them and taking a great many prisoners.

As the news reached Sultan Ahmad's ears, he summoned Qonghartai back. Qonghartai had plotted with Prince Arghun, the eldest son of Abaqa, to betray Sultan Ahmad.

As soon as Sultan Ahmad found out about this collusion, he acted preemptively, and on 28th Shawāl/18th January 1284 in Arran, he had Qonghartai arrested and annihilated.[25]

Ahmad also executed the two other amirs, Kūckak and Shadai Aqtachi, who were in agreement with Qonghartai, and got busy sorting out the other rebels.

* * *

[55]

The reason for mentioning this account was that one day Qonghartai came to the ordu, and in the presence of Ahmad and Qutui Khatun and all the amirs, said: "Tomorrow when Ahmad and Arghun do battle, my retainers and I will withdraw to a private place and we will not take part in the fight."

After that he retired to his winter quarters. The gossip mongers and slanderers took the opportunity to whisper poisoned words to Ahmad and

25 Literally 'nothinged' *nīst gardānīd*.

claimed, "Qonghartai has shared your women in the same way that your own kids and amirs have" and the like.

Meanwhile Kuchak came snooping all around Ahmad's ordu, ten days before Qonghartai. People told Ahmad that Kuchak had come spying and that he had come to gather intelligence about what was happening in the ordu in order to inform Qonghartai.

Because Ahmad's ears had been filled with such ideas, he ordered that his men should seize Qonghartai, a command which they carried out at midday of Wednesday 28th Shawāl 682 (19th January 1284) and that same night Qonghartai's back was broken. This was in accordance with the precepts of Chinggis Khan who had said that the back of whosoever plots against the kingdom should be broken.

Afterwards they interrogated Kuchak and asked him what Qonghartai and Arghun had conspired to do. He said he did not know. They beat him with a cane a hundred times but still he did not confess.

When this was reported to Ahmad, he said: "Kuchak is an old man, a deceiver and a bastard and never tells the truth. Kill him and his son."

[56]

Kuchak and his son were both said to be *gakamashī*. This is a term used among the Mongols when they want to kill someone. If the person says "Kākū", which is the name of a bird, he will not be killed. It is well known among Mongols that should they put that person to death, the killer will be cursed. So Ahmad ordered that they should execute Kuchak but that his son should be spared.

For the next seven days after Qonghartai's killing, an armed force formed a *nerge* standing guard around the ordu. And because the reason for these killings was the victims' friendship with Arghun, it was realised that Arghun was going to retaliate and it was thought best to muster the troops and embark on war against Arghun.

First to arrive was Tubat who was the nephew of Ahmad and the son of Tabshīn, with Prince Baṡar (Yasar), who was also of royal birth.[26]

Alinaq and Māzūq and Shadai, the son of Suqunjaq, and Āchū Sokarchī with eight thousand riders rode out from the region of Mansuriya in Arran.

* * *

On 9th Dhu'l-Qa'dah 682 (29th January 1284), after three days, there was severe snow and due to the difficulty of the road, Tubat and Baṡar (Yasar),

26 Brother of the Chaghadaid prince, Baraq.

who were riding alongside Alinaq, fell behind; and they sent an envoy ahead to announce this delay. Ahmad commented on how slowly they were moving.

Alinaq, along with 200 men, reached the neighbourhood of Ray and attacked a group of people who were part of Arghun's court, robbed them, and then returned to Qazvin with his followers.

[57] year 683/1283–84

When Arghun heard the news, he mobilised with six thousand riders and made Yula Temur [*Yūlā Tāmūr and Yūlā Timūr*][27] the commander of the army.

Hulechu was Tubat and Alinaq's *kachakeh*,[28] namely the army that is behind the advance guard, and Ṭījū and Tekanā followed with ten thousand riders. In the rear came Ahmad, who left Pilsuvar [*Bīlsavār*],[29] which is in Mughan, on Wednesday 8th Safar 683 (26th April 1284) with eight *tūmān* of troops – a *tūmān* is ten thousand.

On Monday 13th Safar (1st May 1284) an envoy from Tubat arrived to announce that Arghun's army had been sighted [in Talaqan].

The next day, another envoy arrived and brought the same news. From the neighbourhood of Ardabil, Ahmad sent Qurumshi, the son of Alinaq, to his father with the message that "If you are greater in number, then fight; and if they are more then you, wait for us to arrive."

Ahmad then left behind his heavy baggage, and on the day of Saturday 18th Safar (6th May 1284) he departed in haste from Ardabil with the army, and every day he covered two stages.

Thursday 16th Safar (4th May 1284), after midday, under the influence of the star sign, Virgo, Arghun clashed until sunset with Tubat and Alinaq in Jamālābād near Qazvin, which the Mongols call Āq Khwājeh, and some groups from both armies fled the battlefield.

[58]

Arghun slept one night on the battlefield while some of his people from the village of Jamālābād, located about ten *farsangs* from the battle, were forced to flee from Tubat's army.

On Monday 20th Safar (8th May 1284) Tubat's envoy reached Ahmad's camp and he brought glad tidings that "We have fought Arghun and he has fled and we have taken many prisoners from his army. The rearguard (*gäjigä* / *kachakeh*) never caught up with us" [pp. 1137–38]. Ahmad was angry

27 Yūlā Tāmūr's son, Baqā'ī, was one of Mustawfī's informants.

28 Rearguard or reserve troops.

29 A town in the province of Arran.

because he knew about this setback from Tekanā. That day they celebrated and made merry.

The next day, Ahmad reached Zangān, and on Thursday 23rd Safar (11th May 1284) he joined Tubat in Sharviyāz and that day they celebrated and made merry.

The next day, prince Huleju[30] was dispatched with a tūmān (10,000) of troops in the direction of Ray, while Ahmad and his commanders positioned themselves in Sharviyāz for two days.

On Monday 27th Safar (15th May) news arrived that Prince Gaykhatu had set out from the vicinity of Hamadan on the pretext of hunting and fled to Khorasan with a few of his people.

The next day (Tuesday, 16th May) Ahmad left his wife, Armini Khatun, in Sharviyāz and set off. On the same day Jushkab[31] arrived from the direction of Baghdad.

The next day (29th Safar/17th May) Ahmad reached Āq Khwājeh [*near Qazvin*], which was the site of the battle of Jamālābād.

The next day they reached Qazvin and reviewed the army. That day Lagzi [*Lakzī*],[32] the son of Arghun Aqa together with Ordu Buqa son of Nawruz, arrived from Arghun's presence. They delivered their khan's apologies, saying: "How can I draw a sword in my Āghā's face? It was never in my mind. But when Alinaq attacked me and plundered, I came to see if he had arrayed his army against me. It was necessary for me to do battle."

[59]

Later that night Lagzi secretly separated from Ordu Buqa, and together they pledged allegiance, and [promised that] Lagzi would remain on the side of Ahmad and that he would keep them informed of all developments in Arghun's camp.

* * *

On Sunday 4th of Rabīᶜ al-Aval (21st May 1284), Ahmad sent Arghun's messengers back. Following them on Monday 5th Rabīᶜ al-Aval (22nd May 1284) he sent Tuq Temūr, the son of Abdallah Āghā (general of Abaqa) and

30 Twelfth son of Hulegu, son of concubine in Dokuz Khatun's ordu.

31 Son of Jumqur, son of Hulegu. He arrived in Iran with Qutui Khatun just after Hulegu's death. Ahmad had assigned him duties in Baghdad.

32 Lagzi Gürägän, son of the former governor of Iran (1243–55), the Oiyat Amir Arghun Aqa [d.1278]. Lagzi married Hulegu's seventh daughter, Baba. His brother Nawruz [d.1297], married Abaqa's daughter, Toghanchuq and was instrumental in the conversion of Ghazan Khan [r.1295–1304] to Islam.

Temur to be there when Arghun should ask his sons to come and sit down together saying such and such and suggest that they all sort things out. "And if Arghun cannot come, let him send Yula Temur and [*the Grand Amir*] Shishi Bakhshi and Qadān and his sons." Behind these emissaries, Ahmad moved forward with the army.

On Wednesday 14th Rabīᶜ al-Aval (31st May 1284), ambassadors returned and they brought the princes, Ghazan [*Qazān*] (r.1295–1304) the son of Arghun Khan, and Prince Omar the son of [Ahmad] Tegudar Yaghī, and the amirs Noghai Yarghuchi,[33] Shishi Bakhshi, and Qadān.[34]

These amirs suggested that the king, Ahmad, withdraw from that locality so that Arghun himself would be prepared to come, "For at this moment the king is angry and he, Arghun, is afraid." Ahmad did not listen and did not retreat, despite the fact that the amirs considered it advisable that he should withdraw. Though his army had been weakened, whenever anyone mentioned this to Ahmad he would reply that he would advance. "Let anyone who wishes come with me; if they do not, let them withdraw."

[60]

The next day, 16th Rabīᶜ al-Aval (2nd June), Ahmad sent back Arghun's amirs and the following day, Saturday (17th Rabīᶜ al-Aval/3rd June), he arrived in Girdeh, and in that place he took recreation and promenade. It was from there that Ahmad dispatched the sons of Prince Taghai Temur, who was a brother of Ahmad, and Sogai, son of Prince Yoshmut; and from among the amirs he sent Buqa Āghā[35] and Doladāī Yarghuchi. Ahmad told Buqa Āghā that he must bring back Arghun and if he would not come, he should bring back Gaykhatu [r.1291–95] together with the amirs whom Ahmad had himself sent back. Buqa Āghā set off and found Arghun in Khuchān.

Ahmad arrived in Damghan with the army on Sunday (18th Rabīᶜ al-Aval/4rd June) and the town was pillaged. Ahmad did not forbid this plundering of Damghan for the reason that his army became debilitated.

33 Noghai Yarghuchi is of the Baya'ut tribe, and he was connected through marriage with the royal family. As a yarghuchi, a judge, he presided over disputes and rifts among the ruling classes.

34 It is not clear who this amir is. Qadan, Guyuk's brother, was serving with Qubilai; Shishi Bakhshi was associated with Sönitäi Noyan and his sons including Emgächin, and the infamous and ambitious Ṫaghājār [Taghachar] Noyan.

35 Buqa son of the Jalayir Ögöläi Qorchi, executed 1289 after prestigious career as vizier then Chingsang under Arghun. He first served under Abaqa with his brother Aruq.

And when they arrived at Kharraqān, Bulghān, who was the *shaḥna* of Shiraz, together with Jurghudāī, who was an amir of a thousand, came to pay homage to Ahmad and they declared themselves *īl*.

The next day, 23rd Rabī' I (9th June), Ahmad sent Alinaq from Kharraqān to Menkalī with Ṭutāq, an amir of a thousand, Qara Buqa, the son of Altajū, and three thousand men. The next day, Ahmad went.

Tuesday 27th Rabīᶜ I, (13th June 1284) the envoy Buqa Āghā arrived in order to collect Prince Gaykhatu.

After a day or so, the final day of Rabīᶜ I, Buqa Āghā arrived, bringing Prince Gaykhatu with him. Ahmad asked Buqa Āghā, "Why didn't you bring back any of the amirs who had returned earlier?" Buqa Āghā said: "I didn't understand that the pādeshāh wanted them." It was for this reason that Ahmad was angry with Buqa Āghā.

After that, Ahmad left Gaykhatu with Tutāī Khatun[36] in Kalpush near Jājaram. From that place, he mustered the army and set off for Quchan, and they did not take one woman with them.

[61]

As soon as Arghun heard that Ahmad was coming, he retraced his steps. When Ahmad arrived in Quchan (9th Rabīᶜ II/25th June), his troops devastated that city. Then after they passed from that place, Arghun with about 100 people made for Kalat Kuh castle situated in Astav near Tus.

Meanwhile Lagzi, who had pledged himself to Ahmad, attacked and pillaged the house of Arghun's wife, Qutlugh Khatun. In the same way Arghun when he had first started fighting Alinaq, had sent someone to the Qara'unas[37] and they had flocked to his, Arghun's support. Then when they heard that Arghun had been defeated, they turned around and every town that lay in their path, they attacked and pillaged.

When Ahmad had passed through the city of Quchan, Lagzi's wife, Baba, who was the sister of Abaqa Khan, came to offer homage to Ahmad. It was also on that day that there was rejoicing when Ahmad was informed that Arghun had fled to Kalat Kuh castle. Alinaq and his retainers with a small army went in pursuit of Arghun in order to prevent him leaving the castle.

36 A much sought-after lady, who began life as a concubine of Abaqa's.

37 The Qara'unas are also called the Negudaris. Originally formed under Sali Noyan in the 1250s to protect the eastern border against the Delhi Sultanate, they later fell under the sway of fleeing Jochid troops, loyal to the Golden Horde. They remained renegade loosely allied with the Chaghadaid khans in later decades based in Khorasan. In 1279 Abaqa brought them to submission and some were rewarded with lands in the west.

The Qara'unas had now become estranged from Arghun, and for this reason it was not possible to escape in that direction, so it was necessary to come out on the same side from which he had entered the fortress.

Alinaq with his army, presuming that Arghun would come to fight, made preparation for war.

[62]

Arghun sent Altāī to Alinaq's lines saying: "I am coming to see Ahmad." After that, with Bulaghan [*Bulaghān*] Khatun and other royal ladies, Arghun presented himself before Ahmad in the Rādkān (rāyekān) meadow on Thursday 13th Rabīᶜ al-Akhar (29th June 30th May 1284).

On the day that Arghun arrived, because Ahmad ascribed a secret motive to his commanders who used to speak about Arghun in such a way that it would lead to ill-will, he faced all the top amirs and demanded of them, "Now, whose claim was right?" No one could say anything.

Buqa Āghā said happily, "My Happy King, your words were right."

He said, "Since my words were right, tomorrow we will go before 'Ātū'," that is his mother Qutui Khatun. "Let everyone prepare their own speeches." All the amirs, and especially, Buqa Āghā, feared these words.

On Friday, 14th of the month (Rabīᶜ II, 30th June), Ahmad struck camp and then returned two *farsangs*. Then on Saturday, the rest decamped since that day at Sar-cheshma, Bulaghan Khatun was holding a feast for Ahmad. In the middle of that feast Alinaq, Ṫutāq, and Qarā Buqa said to each other in drunkenness that as long as Ahmad had not killed those princes, his kingship would not be secure.

The night of Sunday, 16th of the month (Rabīᶜ II/2nd July), Ahmad entrusted Arghun to the army charging them with guarding him while Ahmad himself, with 200 horsemen, went to Kalpush, the place where Tutāī Khatun and Gaykhatu were ensconced, since Ahmad had previously sent Gaykhatu to that place.

When Ahmad had gone, Buqa Āghā sent someone to his older brother, Aruq Āghā saying, "Ahmad has plans for us. What is to be done?" Aruq Āghā was with Jushkab.

Aruq said that Qaramush (Qurumshi), the son of Hindu Āghar (Hinduqur),[38] had come and given them the news that during Bulaghan Khatun's feast, Alinaq and others had also had just such a conversation. The brothers, Buqa Āghā and Aruq Āghā, met up with each other and they involved Jushkab in their plans.

38 Rashīd al-Dīn seems to suggest that this is Qurumshi Kuregan, son of Alinaq.

[63]

They befriended Tekanā[39] who had also had suspicions regarding Ahmad, and because Tekanā was with Huleju, they said that they would be prepared to give the crown to Huleju.

In short, all the amirs and princes were in agreement and they were all enjoying the feast during which they encouraged Alinaq to drink wine. Alinaq insisted that since that night it was his watch [*gäzik*] and he had to guard Arghun, he could not drink.

Jushkab said that he would guard Arghun on his behalf. Alinaq trusted him. They got Alinaq drunk and that same night they got Arghun mounted on a horse with Buqa Āghā. Arghun rode direct to the house of Alinaq.

And that very night which was the night of Monday, 17th Rabīᶜ II (3rd July), they made an end of Alinaq and they also killed Ṫuṫāq.[40]

Also that night, someone was sent to Huleju and Tekanā to say: "We have killed Alinaq and Ṫuṫāq. You must kill Baṡar Oghul and Abukān." Because Huleju hated Prince Baṡar (Yasar) but liked Abukān, they killed Prince Baṡar with a bowstring and preserved the latter, Abukān.

On the day of Tuesday 18th Rabī' II (4th July 1284), someone from Ṫuṫāq's unit was near Kūrūī, which was a dependency of Isfarāyīn. At midday, he reached Ahmad and told him that Ṫuṫāq had been killed and there was alarm within the army. The Amir, Aq Buqa,[41] took him to address Ahmad and the soldier explained the situation. They consulted astronomers and inquired about their own circumstances. After that, Ahmad retreated and settled near Isfarāyīn.

The next day, a messenger arrived from Māzuq Āghā to inform Ahmad that his enemies had killed all his supporters and that they were now all united. "If you can, get yourself out."

[64]

The day of Wednesday 19th Rabīᶜ II (5th July 1284), Ahmad fled from the vicinity of Isfarāyīn in the direction of Kalpush. Halfway there at Jājarm, Khwājeh, the ṣāḥib dīwān (Shams al-Dīn Juwaynī) came and informed Ahmad: "We have no animals. If Ahmad permits, I will go to Gūyān (Juwayn) in order to bring a dromedary into service for the desert road

39 This is Amir Tägänä Totqavul, general under Abaqa.

40 Taitaq son of Qubai Noyan was Abaqa Khan's *kükältash*, and Ahmad's amir-ordu. In fact he was not killed and was allowed to escape after his capture.

41 Tenth son of one of Hulegu's chief generals, the Jalayir Elgäi Noyan, excelled under Gaykhatu, killed by Baidu.

to Yazd." Ahmad declared, "Let it be so!" The khwājeh[42] (Shams al-Dīn Juwaynī[43]) separated from Ahmad at that very place, Jājarm, and they were never to meet again. May God have mercy upon them.

When Ahmad arrived at Armini Khatun's ordu in Shariviyār, where Suqunjaq Āghā was waiting, he commanded that the house of Buqa Āghā be plundered.

It was in that region that Ahmad was told that Yula Temur had been captured, "What must be done with him?" He demanded, "Don't you know what must be done? He and his followers must be executed according to the yasa. Despite such crimes as he has committed he came to me and I said to him, go to the ordu of Armini (Khatun) and wait until I come, and he fled." In short, Yula Temur and his dependents were killed.

Ahmad came to Sarāū (Sarāb) to the ordu of Qutui Khatun, where he was joined by about 2000 persons. He wanted to disappear. Sakat (Shiktür Noyan) Āghā and Qarā Noqāī, a son of Prince Yoshmut, said that if he left they would not be able to answer to the princes, amirs, and Arghun. They kept him under observation.

When this large group of rebels reached Kharraqān, they formed an assembly to declare who should be the king. They wanted to know when exactly Ahmad had fled. First they had to decide his fate.

Then Charīk the Mongol was sent with Ṫulāī Yarghūchī to track Ahmad down and behind them went Arghun and Buqa Āghā, and following them, the princes Hulaju and Gaykhatu [r.1291–95] and [the Amir] Tekanā.

[65]

A messenger named Burah was sent to the Qara'unas who were in Suyur laq (*Siyah Kuh*) to inform them that Ahmad had fled. His message said simply, "You should go and plunder the ordus."

The Qara'unas came to the ordu of Qutui Khātūn where they found Ahmad. They plundered the ordu and ordered Ahmad to be handed over to them. Sekat (Shiktūr Āghā) and Qarā Noqāī refused to surrender him and told the invaders, "We will guard him together until Arghun comes."

After that, the talks continued in Tūrghāj where the assembly deliberated over who should be king. Buqa Āghā said Abaqa had bequeathed the throne to Arghun: "After me Arghun will be king." And Dankiz Küregen attested

42 Khwāja/khwajeh can be translated as lord; it is an honorary title awarded respected notables, great merchants, and respected clerics.

43 Without Sultan Ahmad's support, the Juwaynī brothers had little defence against their powerful enemies among whom was Arghun Khan and both were dead within a short time of Ahmad's demise.

to this since in the Mongol *yasa* there is no clear ruling on imperial bequests [*hīch beh jāī vasiyyat nīstand*]. Also, Arghun was liked by both the great lords and the army of the Qara'unas, so they agreed upon that.

On Tuesday 24th Jumādī al-Aval 683 (8th August 1284), Ahmad was tried for the killing of Qonghartai, and he had no excuse for that deed. On the night of Wednesday, 25th Jumādī al-Aval (9th August 1284) they killed Ahmad, in the same way that Ahmad had killed Qonghartai.

On Friday, 27th Jumādī al-Aval (10th August 1284), the king of the world, Arghun, was seated on the throne with celebration in Ṭāla' Qūs (Sagittarius), may it be happy and auspicious for mortals; may his reign increase and his sovereignty be multiplied, with Muḥammad and his family.

[66]

The night is pregnant, let's see what it gives birth to
Let us wait and see what the finger of the time will touch.
We have seen whatever has come out of the rotation of the sky
And if we live long enough we will see whatever will happen in the future.

3 An annotated translation

The *Akhbār-i-Moghūlān dar Anbāneh-ye Quṭb*

Akhbār-i-Moghūlān dar Anbāneh-ye Quṭb by Quṭb al-Dīn Shīrāzī, edited by Īraj Afshār, Qum: Grand Library of Āyatollah Mar'ashī Najafī, 2010/1389

Beginning of the Mongol government and the appearance of Chinggis Khan

Bin Yīsūkā bin Qubilā bin Sanqū Bahādar was in the year 599 Hijri, [1202] in the reckoning of the Rumiyans the year 1514, in the reckoning of the Yazdjardi 572, in the Uyghur date [*Tonghuz 'Yil* – Turkish] the year of the Pig, and in the Chinese [*Khiṭā'yān*] date the year of the Pig [*kuy*].

[*Temujin was the son of Yesugei, the son of Bartan Baghutar son of Kabul Khan, the Qa'an under the Jurchens. He was the son of Tembinai son of the great Qaidu who, it is claimed, first had the ambition to unite the Turco-Mongol tribes.*]

Early accounts of Temüjin record events in Wadi Baljuna [*Wādī Bālchūneh*],[1] which is close to the lands of the Chinese. [*This is the only time that Baljuna is referred to as a river valley. It is called a river, a lake, or simply a place and its nature remains controversial. See de Rachewiltz,* ***Secret History****, p. 655.*] His followers had gone without food for a few days, when one amongst them succeeded in shooting down a desert sparrow. The bird was cooked and then it was presented to their leader. Temüjin ordered that the bird be divided equally into 70 portions, and from that he took his own share that was no larger than any of the other portions. It was because of his willingness to share the tribulations of his men and because of his righteousness that people became his devotees and followers and were prepared to surrender their souls to him.

1 Where possible the more standard form of proper names has been used with the transliteration of the Persian form as used by Shīrāzī in square brackets.

[Wadi Baljuna was a decisive turning point in Temujin's career. He had suffered a major defeat and had been abandoned by all but his most devoted followers. All who were with him during the hard times at Wadi Baljuna would later be rewarded for their faith and steadfastness. This episode recounting the magical feeding of the seventy is mentioned in no other source.][2]

Page 20 of the Persian edition

From his offspring there were four famous sons who became renowned among the people: Chaghatai [Jaghatāī] Khan, Ögötei [Hūkatāī] Khan, Tolui [Tūlī] Khan, and Jochi [Tūshī] Khan.

Chaghatai did not live long after his father, and Chinggis Khan appointed Ögötei king in his own lifetime and he placed his son in the position of his own deputy.

He appointed Jochi Khan to the provinces of Qipchaq [Khifjāq], Rus [Rūs], Saqsin and Bulgar and his descendants ruled there.

The first was Ghūnkarān, after him came Shībān Khan, then Batu Khan, then Berke, then Möngke Temur [Monkū Timūr], and then Tuta Mongke [Tūtā Monkū], who is Shah at present, **[end of facsimile 22b]** that is in 680/1281–2.

[Jochi who died in 1227 had a number of sons Orda (Ghunkaran), Shiban, Batu, and Berke. Orda Ichen 1204–1251, the eldest took command of the White Horde, Batu took command of the Blue Horde, while Shiban had lands in the far north. Batu with Orda's agreement assumed command of the more powerful armies of the Jochi or Qipchaq Khanate later known as the Golden Horde.]

After that was the branch of Ögötei Qa'an, who was succeeded by Güyük Khan.

When Güyük died, in consultation with and on the advice of Batu Khan, Möngke Qa'an was enthroned; and the sons of Chaghatai and Ögötei who were not pleased with that decision plotted opposition, and resolved on action against Möngke Khan.

Möngke Khan[3] became aware of their schemes and resolved to meet their machinations with justifiable, considered (*rā'ī ṣowāb va indīsheh-ye ṣāfī*), and decisive retaliation. Such was the scale of his retaliation with killing, beating, shackling, and the like that not one person from those that

2 Comments, explanations, and references to passages in Rashīd al-Dīn have also been enclosed in square brackets. Sentences which appear verbatim in Rashīd al-Dīn appear italicized in the text.

3 No explanation is offered for the switch from using Qa'an to Khan.

had been accomplices in insubordination was exempted, though not one innocent person suffered loss.

The like of the justice and equity in the time of Möngke Khan had seldom existed before. During his time the wolf and the sheep would drink water together.

Page 21

When Möngke Khan had resolved the affairs of that vast empire (*ān valāiyāt bisyār*), consisting of the provinces of Turkestan, northern China, Transoxiana, Tibet, and Tangut, he sent his own brother Hülegü [Hūlākū] to sort out the lands beyond the Oxus [Jayḥūn], namely the provinces of the Arabs and the Persians (*'arab va 'ajam*).

Page 22, year 650 odd/1252

Hülegü Khan came in the year six hundred and fifty-odd to subdue the land from Khorasan until he reached Damascus; and he took all of Khorasan, Jabāl, Kirman, and Ghaznīn until Multan, and much of the country of Hind, and Iraq-i-'Ajam and Iraq-i-'Arab, as well as Mazanderan, and the lands from Arran, Shirwan, and Darband as far as the interior of the Qipchaq steppe. He brought an army from Rus, and with that army plundered the deserts of Arabia. And before [accomplishing all] this, he had [already] seized the caliph of Baghdad himself and taken all the sultans of Diyarbakir and Syria.**[24a]**

And Hülegü became the ruler in Rum and the [land of] the Franks [Palestine]. These lands, which – if anyone heard tell of them, they would be astonished – were open to him in total, that is, from Transoxiana to Damascus, from the deserts of Iraq-i 'Arab to Russia, and from Hind to Khwarazm. We had seen Hülegü in his court enough times to see that in one day he dealt efficiently with the affairs of this province [presumably Azerbaijan] and that in every one of the provinces under his command, he governed well, in such a way that his justice was total wherever was *īl* to him.

[*There is only one meeting between Shīrāzī and Hulegu recorded in other sources and for this reason doubt has been cast on Shīrāzī's authorship of this chronicle since this passage suggests regular meetings*.]

When Hülegü had passed over the River Oxus [Jayḥūn], he arrived in Khorasan. After that he assembled around himself many armies from Turkestan, northern China [Khiṭā] and Transoxiana with men and armaments beyond count, such as the '*Kamān-hā-ye cherkh*,' a crossbow that drew three bows with one string.

[*See also Howorth p. 97; (Jūzjānī) Raverty p. 1191; Raverty fails to clarify where he found the passage which describes the crossbow and weapons in terms and words similar to this. However, Peter Jackson throws light on this and on the nature of these armaments in his definitive study of the Chinggisids in the Islamic West. His descriptions of the weapons are refreshingly clear.*[4]]

Page 23

[Every] Three bows fired one arrow and each of their arrows was nearly three-quarters of a *gaz* [approx. metre] in length including the point. The shaft of the point came up to the notch of the arrow and the feather extended from the notch to the point, such that they had attached the feather of a vulture or an eagle to the shaft of the arrow.

["*From the towers bows sent up swift-feathered shafts, and a Kamān-i-gāv, which had been constructed by Khitayan craftsmen and had a range of 2,500 paces, was brought to bear on those fools, when no other remedy remained; and of the devil-like Heretics many soldiers were burnt by those meteoric shafts." Juwaynī, Boyle, pp. 630–31; Qazvīnī, p. 128. Ox's bow, literally; a ballista or magnified crossbow which propelled javelins rather than stones.*]

All arrows were turned, not shaved, with a plane or a knife, and the mangonel arrows were made from white poplar wood and enclosed in the skin of horse and cow rind [*gāv barash*] in the same way as the scabbard of a knife or sword is covered. Of these mangonel arrows, on every mangonel five or seven are tied together and set with putty (*baṭān-hā*) [Iraj Afshar's footnote says an unusual word possibly meaning cotton].

All these machines were brought from Turkestan on vehicles with skilled and competent operatives. And from that locality, namely the border of Khorasan, Hülegü Khan ordered decrees to be written and messengers dispatched to the rulers and kings of the provinces, saying: "I am setting out **[24b]** against the Heretics [*Mulahida*].[5] If you send assistance in the form of troops and armaments, provisions and military supplies, I will count it as a favour and your province will have peace and security. But if you neglect to do this, as soon as I become free from my present concerns, I will deal with you and after that no excuses or apology will be acceptable."

4 Peter Jackson, *The Mongols and the Islamic World* (New Haven and London: Yale University Press, 2017), pp. 136–137.

5 "Shīrāzī" does not use this term himself, here putting it in the mouth of Hulegu. He uses the term Ismā'īliyān.

Page 24

So, in response, they came: kings like the Atābek of Fārs Muẓaffer al-Dīn Abū Bakr bin Saᶜd and the sultans of Rum ʻIzz al-Dīn and Rukn al-Dīn; as well as the rulers of Khorasan, Sistan, Mazanderan, Kirman, Rustamdār, Sherwān, Georgia [Gurjistān], Iraq, Azerbaijan, Arran, Lurestan, and more, some accompanied by their own people.

The remainder, who did not come in person, sent brothers and relatives with armies, provisions, supplies, ceremony (*takalluf-hā*), servants, and their allegiance and gifts to serve their new king.

[*Rashīd al-Dīn's longer account (p. 979) contains similarities to this report with shared details suggesting a common source. The report in Mustawfī's* Żafarnāma p. 20 *calling on the Iranians to harken to his call resembles this account closely.*]

From all the provinces, Hülegü's commanders arranged the distribution of provisions and supplies without limit and beyond compare transported by donkey, camel, cow, asses ["long ears"], and such like. Such was the organisation that noodles, cooked porridge, and pounded millet [*gāvrus-i kufteh*] had been brought from the provinces of Northern China and Uyghuristan [Yughorestān] to the foot of Alamut and Mīmūndaz and that castle, Girdkūh; and every half *farsang* they had stacked so much flour, rice, and necessities (staples) in bags of fine linen [that] everywhere great hills appeared.

Page 25, year 651–1253/4

From Khorasan, Hülegü sent his massed armies to Qohestan. First, in Rabīᶜ al-Aval of the year 651/May 1253, he sent an army to the foot of Girdkūh and he overcame the fortifications, the like of which [*saftī*] no one has ever seen.

They dug a huge moat surrounding the castle, and behind the moat they built a fortified wall, and after the wall they built sheltered houses, and after the houses they built another wall and another moat after that.**[32a]** In this way, if anyone from inside the castle attempted to break out, or if anyone from outside planned to break in, in order to relieve the people within the castle, the moats and the fortified walls would act as a deterrent from both directions.

Hülegü Khan himself went to the foot of the castle and for one or two days conducted the battle. Because these measures against the defenders of the castle were not proving easy, he assigned the entire army to that place and the grandest commanders were appointed to this campaign.

Page 26

And after approximately one year, cholera struck and a great many of the people of the castle died. The news was taken to ᶜAlā' al-Dīn Moḥammad, pādeshāh of the Ismā'īlīs, informing him that not one man remained in the castle of Girdkūh and it would invariably be lost. 'Alā' al-Dīn sent 100 men under the army commander, Moqdam al-Dīn Moḥammad Mobāraz in order to break through the cordon and allow his squadron to pass through that body of men that were besieging the castle. None of that company of men apart from one man who fell into the moat and broke his leg but who was safely removed, was injured.

And those 100 men reached the castle and they were able to work at strengthening the fortifications and for nearly 20 years that castle remained besieged. However, finally, when the defenders surrendered, all of them were killed.

[*Rashīd al-Dīn (pp. 981–82) has a similar story though he provides more detail. Names and figures agree and it is likely that the two accounts originated from a common source.*]

Page 27, year 653/1255

In Zū al-Q'adeh of the year 653/December 1255, an apostate who had become a special retainer of the Khwarshāh [Khūrshāh], and on whom he relied, killed ᶜAlā' al-Dīn Moḥammad.

[*Rashīd al-Dīn (pp. 982–83) reports this incident but provides far more detail including the claim that Rukn al-Dīn was directly responsible for the assassination of his father and then later of the assassin, Ḥasan Mazanderanī himself. Shīrāzī as a Shi'ite himself might not have been so willing to attack the reputation of another Alid, albeit an Ismā'īlī.*]

His son, Rukn al-Dīn Ḥasan, whom they called Khwarshāh, took the throne in place of his father. Rukn al-Dīn Ḥasan sent a brother named Shāhanshāh to the presence of Hülegü so that he could declare that: "though my father was not *īl*, I am *īl* and willing to serve you."

[*'īl' is a Mongol word adopted by Iranians which expresses the idea of loyalty, trust-worthiness, obedience and willingness to serve.*]

This Shāhanshāh went to Nishapur and arrived to present himself before Hülegü. He was seized and taken to Iraq.

Rukn al-Dīn sent another prince **[32b]** who would offer homage. "Let him [Hülegü] send my brother back from the province of Ray so that he can appear before us again." Though the brother had left with 200 men, he was returned with only ten persons and a terse command, "Go ! If Rukn al-Dīn cannot come himself, he should send us another brother or son."

Page 28

On the advice of his wazir, [Khwāja Aṣīl al-Dīn Zozanī],[6] Rukn al-Dīn sent another brother named Shīrānshāh with a number of rare gifts. But when Hülegü said, "Since you have become *īl*, be secure", the conqueror was

6 Named in Rashīd al-Dīn, p. 986, unreadable in *Akhbār*, p. 23 alef.

thinking, "they are unaware that our army has appeared in their province." When the Ismā'īlīs sent a representative to speak with those Mongol amirs, asking "We have become *īl*, why then have you come to our lands?" Those amirs answered "since a state of submission (*īlī*) and concord now exists, we have come to graze our horses."

[*Though in later paragraphs there are closer similarities sometimes verbatim between Rashīd al-Dīn and 'Shīrāzī', the accounts sometimes mirror each other, in the following extract word for word. yeganegi ast ma beh 'alef khwar amadeh 'im yeganegi masluk ast beh 'alef khwar amadeh 'im. Unfortunately, the sloppy grammar and writing make the Shīrāzī document difficult to comprehend and follow without reference to Rashīd al-Dīn.*]

As soon as Hülegü reached the border of their province, he fell upon them with thundering hooves. If it had not been for the excessive rainfall that night, it is possible that they would have captured Rukn al-Dīn at the foot of the castle.

[*This sentence appears in Rashīd al-Dīn with a couple of synonymous words used in place of others, i.e. dastgīr shudeh instead of begereftand, besīār instead of az kaśrat.*]

However, Rukn al-Dīn, realising the danger of his situation, returned to the castle at daybreak.

In one hour, armies arrived from every direction, surrounding the castle in numbers no one until that time had ever seen. They could not believe that such numbers of men as they witnessed were possible to muster, for Hülegü's armies had so occupied mountain, thicket, and plain that in no direction was there a path for a single foot-soldier. In less than a night and day all around the castle that rose like a mighty mountain, the besieging army had formed a *nerge* that encircled the castle for a distance of approximately six *farsangs*.

[*See Rashīd pp. 484–6.*]

After 13 days, with the approval and consultation of the nobles and ministers of his government, Rukn al-Dīn emerged from his castle and went to prostrate himself before Hülegü. When Hülegü saw him, he realised that he was a child **[23a]** and lacked experience and guile [*kafāyatī*]. He reassured the Khwarshāh with sweet words, and sent someone to evacuate all the castellans and people from all the forts that they possessed in Khorasan, Qumis, Rudbar and Syria. The result was that they surrendered all the castles, which numbered more than a hundred, apart from Girdkūh, which has itself been mentioned and which remained under siege for about 20 years, and the fortress of Lamasar, in which there were relatives of Rukn al-Dīn and which they preserved for more than a year. Though the people of that fortress perished of pestilence and sickness, nobody emerged from any of the other castles, which were more than 100, with even a nose bleed.

Finally, he sent Rukn al-Dīn to see Möngke Qa'an.

Page 29

When they brought him to a place where he was allowed to be by himself, it was there that he was killed. Between Qazvin and Abhar, the remaining brothers, his children, the women of his harem, and his dependents were killed and that [Ismā'īlī] state ceased to exist.

[*Rashīd al-Dīn elaborates and explains that Mongke Qa'an was annoyed that so much time and man power had been wasted on this petulant boy (p. 991) and Juwayni provides far more detail of the events that transpired (Boyle, pp. 722–25; Qazvīnī, vol.III, pp. 74–78).*]

Page 30, year 655/1257

From that place, at the beginning of the year 655/1257, Hülegü busied himself with the group of kings and the people of the Jibāl, as for example in Tang, Kulīn, and Īveh and such places, and carried them off.

In Shawāl 655/October 1257, he mounted his horse and set off from Hamadan for Baghdad, which he reached in three months. Every day he travelled no more than two *farsangs*. He organised his armies in such a way that from the province of Fars until the province of Rum, one body of men without limit and number descended upon Baghdad.

The army of Fars and Kirman came by way of Khuzestan and Shushtar. It was such that the army's left wing came by the shores of the Sea of Oman and the right wing **[23b]** had merged with their troops from Iraq and the rest. The army of Rum proceeded from the border of Syria and Diyarbakr in such a way that their left wing joined with the armies of Arran and Azerbaijan while at the same time they poured from all sides into Iraq-i-'Arab. The first party to reach Baghdad and confront the army of Baghdad was commanded by Prince Buqa Temur, Baiju Noyan [Bāyjū Nū^cīn], and Suqunjaq Noyan [Sūnjāq Nū^cīn]. They say *noyan* for *amir* in the Mongol language.

Page 31

Each one of these amirs had 10 or 15 thousand men. In Baghdad they reached the Jarīt [*Nahr Isa, mentioned in Rashīd al-Dīn*]. The Caliph's army, whose leader and commander was Mujāhad al-Dīn Bebakaraz [*both Rashīd al-Dīn and Juwaynī name this official* 'Aybak'. *His title dawātdār means 'keeper of the (royal) inkwell' and he was a minister of state, the chamberlain.*] Dawātdār, whom they called the Lesser [*kūchuk*] Dawātdār, who was the axis [*modār*] of the army and the government of the caliph Musta'ṡim bil'allah Abū Aḥmad, went to confront the enemy army and their vanguard, which comprised four or five thousand men and which was commanded by

Suqunjaq Noyan. The Dawātdār's army struck the Mongol forces and completely routed them and forced them to retreat four *farsangs* from the regions of Dajīl to Bashīriyeh, and when night came Suqunjaq's forces remained in that very same place and the army of Baghdad did not enter the town.

For two nights Suqunjaq maintained contact with (*khabar kard*) that army that Buqa Temur and Baiju commanded, while they meanwhile made their way to join Suqunjaq. They sent their own armies to surround the [Caliph's] armies of Baghdad, and as dawn broke, they raised a shout and put hands to sword. They say that the army of Baghdad was drowned in the sea.

[*Rashīd al-Dīn provides the background and detail and an explanation for the fate of Baghdad's army. While Suqunjaq and according to Rashīd, Buqa Temur, were licking their wounds in Bashīriyeh, they were joined by Baiju, and together they opened the dykes of Baghdad's canal and irrigation system thereby flooding the whole region including the area into which they then drove the Caliph's forces. pp. 1011–12.*]

The Dawātdār with a troop of horsemen fell upon the invaders and escaped [back to Baghdad] while a group of famished Turks who had broken out in a different direction escaped in the direction of Syria.

Hülegü approached from the direction of the Khorasan Road, and from the Dawātdār's army the slain **[25a]** were retrieved and from them 12,000 ears were severed. These ears were sent to Hülegü, but this total excluded the ears of those who had fled from the battlefield and had then fallen into the water and streams.

[*While Rashīd al-Dīn provides far more detail including the 12,000 dead, he omits mention of the gift of ears for Hulegu. He also recounts that the Dawatdār made his way back to Baghdad while others fled to Hilla and Kufa though no mention is made of those Baghdadi soldiers who escaped capture but failed to return to the Caliph's service as being 'hungry Turks'. pp. 1011–12.*]

Page 32

When Hülegü reached Baghdad the rest of his army, who were already in the city, was standing on the ramparts. Because a great assemblage of people, namely all the people of the Sawād, had come to the city before the Mongol army arrived, there was a great dearth, want, and scarcity of provisions in Baghdad. Pestilence [*wabā*] struck and many people died. The number of deaths reached the point that the Ministry's [*Bayt al-māl*] priority was to prepare the corpses and bury them. Meanwhile the situation deteriorated so much that the people of Baghdad could no longer cope with ablutions and burial of the dead, so bodies were thrown into the Tigris. In the end, it became so bad that they could not even carry the dead to the Tigris on account of the number who were dying, as the porters did not have time and were no longer turning up. At this point the caliph commanded that an empty property be assigned for each area and the dead be put there and as it filled and as they found the opportunity, they would bury them. Even when the army arrived, they were unable to cope with the situation.

[*This is the only source which mentions pestilence as a major cause of death in the stricken city and later, it reports that many of the invaders including Hulegu were afflicted by this sickness. Rashīd al-Dīn alludes only to the foul air, p. 1017, and the fact that Hulegu had been 'unwell' p. 1020. However, in the account attributed to Ibn Fowaṭī, it is acknowledged that an epidemic attacked the survivors of the Mongol attack; "Those that survived the killing were struck by an epidemic from breathing the odour of corpses and drinking contaminated water. The inhabitants frequently smelled onions because of the strong smell" p. 368.*[7]]

Hülegü reached the city of Baghdad and ordered the erection of mangonels. He set up a single tower carrying 16 mangonels at the Aleppo Gate and the Gate of Triumph. They hurled rocks of 100 to 5 *mann* and during one day and night they pulverised the stronghold that they called the Persian [ᶜ*Ajamī*] Tower.

Because mangonel stone could not be found in the vicinity of Baghdad, **[25b]** they brought rocks from Jelūlā and Jabal al-Ḥamrīn. They cut up palm trees with handsaws and hurled them with the mangonel.

[*This sentence appears verbatim in Rashīd al-Dīn, p. 1013, lines 7–8.*]

When the people grew afraid, the caliph sought quarter and announced, "We will make peace and we will surrender."

Hülegü commanded that the Mongols that had gone to the top of the battlements should not descend. "They must remain there until they [the caliph's advisers] emerge!" He sent a message saying, "If you are *īl* send out the army so that we can count them and in due course we can seek out people who may be useful to us."

Page 33

The caliph ordered that his army should go outside to surrender and Hülegü sent a *yarliq* and *paiza* for the commanders of the caliph's army, first the Dawātdār and afterwards Sulīmānshāh and the rest, saying, "Let them come forth and bring their troops, so that when I go to Syria they may provide assistance".

7 Hend Gilli-Elewy, "Al-Ḥawādiṯ al-gāmiʿa: A Contemporary Account of the Mongol Conquest of Baghdad, 656/1258", *Arabica*, Vol. 58 (2011), pp. 353–371, p. 368.

When the army of Baghdad resolved to come out, countless people from those who were not military or army also came out. They supposed that in so far as they came forth they might find safety, and it would be worse in the city. In fact, the opposite was true, for those in the city who remained hidden in holes, furnaces, and dark places remained safe and unharmed, while those who came outside were divided up and distributed into 10,000s [*tūmānī*], 1000s, 100, and 10s and they were all killed. It was thus since Hülegü had commanded that they be counted and 1,022,000 humans were slain.

They brought out the caliph after Hülegü had entered the city and feasted in his palace. Hülegü's court decamped from the city to a village that they call Waqaf. Then they came outside the city.

Page 34, events of the year 656/1258

[On the] day . . . [at the time of the] afternoon prayer . . .[8] in the year 656/1258 they martyred the caliph, and they martyred his two eldest sons – whether before or after him, is not known – and the armies returned from there. The weather had become warm and the great stench penetrated the brains of the people.

Pestilence struck and most of the Mongol army became sick, and many died of the disease. They came to the provinces of Sīāh Kūh and Hamadan.

Hülegü became sick for 20 days and then he became well.

[*Hulegu decamped from Baghdad on Wednesday 14th Safar (20th Feb) on account of the foul air. . . . He had been unwell but he recovered (Rashīd al-Dīn, pp. 1020).*]

He went to Arran and Mūqān for the winter, and at the end of the winter he sent the army with his son Yoshmūt to Diyarbakir. They went and lay siege to Mayyāfāriqīn. Yoshmūt returned at the beginning of summer.

Page 35, year 657 (1258/59)

In the spring of this year, that is the year 657/1258, Hülegü went himself to Syria and conquered all the country of Diyarbakir and Syria. They killed the greater number of the people of Aleppo; and the people of Damascus sent messengers and gifts, and Sultan Malek Nāsir had left to avoid war. The Sultan had gone in the direction of Egypt and Yemen.

8 There is a blank space in these two positions on the original ms.

Hülegü had sent a *shahneh*[9] and governor to Damascus, 'Alā' al-Dīn Jāstī (Hashi) and Qāḍī Shams al-Dīn Qomī.[10] [*Rashīd al-Dīn includes an unnamed Mongol shaḥna and another Tajik governor, Jamāl al-Dīn Qaraqai Qazvīnī, p. 1027.*] It was surprising that many of the people of Damascus were generally Yazīdī (derogatory term for Sunni)[11] and each of these were Qomī Shi'ites.[12] The people of Damascus were so happy with them that not for one moment did any affliction disturb these two great ones. [*ghabārī beh īn dū bozorg naresīd.*]

Page 36, year 658 (1259–60)

In the year 658/1259–60 there were few amirs in rank and status greater than Ket Buqa Noyan, around whom the Mongol army revolved, **[26b]** and there was no one greater in manliness or judgement, and after him victory nowhere never again fell to the Mongol army.

He was in Ba'lbek in the summer with one tūmān [10,000 soldiers] of the Mongol army. The troops of Syria and Egypt were all under the Sultanate of Quduz, sultan through his sedition against the Kāmiliyān[13] who had been sultans of Syria and Egypt. They came to be of one language, and assembled in Kerak [Kartak] and Shawbak [Shūyak].[14]

Ket Buqa [Ked Būqā] had given Baidar [Bāīdar], who was an amir, his own advance guard and had sent him to the Gaza plain.

As Quduz moved on Syria, Baidar sent a message to Ket Buqa saying "Our army is ready, what is your command?"

Ket Buqa cautioned not to take another step back until he himself arrived. By the time the reply reached Baidar, the army of Quduz was upon

9 A *Shahneh* in Persian, a *Basqaq* in Turkish, and a *Daraghuchi* in Mongolian, and roughly interchangeable terms meaning an overseer or representative of the imperial power, appointed by the Khan to whom he would report back and whose interests he would protect.

10 Rashīd al-Dīn states that there was one Mongol shaḥna and three Tajik liegemen, p. 1027.

11 Yazīd ibn Mu'āwiya ibn Abī Sufyān, 20 July 647–11 November 683, second Umayad Caliph who had Husain killed at the battle of Kerbala, 10 October 680/10 Muharram, 61.

12 Qom is an Iranian holy city, 125 kms south-west of Tehran, which houses the shrine of Fatima al-Mu'sumeh, sister of Ali, Imam Reza (d.818).

13 Ayyubids 1171–1260; al-Malik al-Kamil Naser ad-Din Abu al-Ma'ali Muhammad) (c. 1177–1238) the fourth Kurdish Ayyubid sultan of Egypt. Under sultan Kamīl [Meledin], the Ayyubids defeated the Fifth Crusade but as a result of the Sixth Crusade, he ceded Jerusalem to the Franks and is known to have met with Saint Francis.

14 These were the Mamluks of Cairo who challenged the Ilkhans originally for regional hegemony and later for the leadership of the Islamic world. The Mamluks harboured a claimant to the Abbasid Caliphate. They were ethnic Turks, Qipchaqs-Cumans, Caucasians, Circassians, and even Turco-Mongols sold or captured as slave soldiers.

him and they put him to flight. Ket Buqa arrived and cruelly demanded of him, "Why didn't you stand your ground until you were killed in that same place?"

Page 37

Baidar replied, "I couldn't stand, would you have?"

The next day before dawn the Syrian army came upon Ket Buqa,[15] and not a horse's head turned. Anyone from the army of Ket Buqa who did not flee was killed in that very same place; and Quduz's men chased the remainder from the province of Gaza to the city of Homs and the shores of the river Orontes [ᶜĀṡī]. Ket Buqa [**27a**] was killed in the same place that he was captured. The Syrian and Egyptian army also captured Ket Buqa's sons and wives and other women and boys of his army that were in Ba'lbek and other places in Syria.

Also, in the middle of these altercations and the war, following the instigation and consultation of Rukn al-Dīn Bekodesh Bunduqdār, Quduz Sultan himself was assassinated, along with his retainers and relatives.

Rukn al-Dīn Bekodesh Bunduqdār [Baybars, 1223–1 July 1277] was enthroned as sultan of Egypt and Syria, and with imperial pomp he assumed control of that country. Never before had history witnessed a person that had such judgement and foresight. His first commands were the prohibition of wine, and for notables, military officers, and Turks, the prohibition of assembly and deliberation, and the seizure of all of the cities on the shore of the Farang Sea from Iskandarya [Alexandria] as far as the province of Sīs [ancient capital of Cilician Armenia, south-west of Kozan in Adana Province].

[*Rashīd al-Dīn reports neither the previous nor the following anecdote concerning a Frankish attempt at infiltrating Mamluk territory through deception.*]

On one occasion, 700 Franks conspired to commit acts of deceit [*ḥiylat kārī*] on their Muslim neighbours. They claimed that in a dream their hearts had become so fearful of their Frankish religion and faith that they had become Muslims. "We have come to serve the sultan so that after the religion of Islam has been presented and taught to us, we will be given a place in a school so that we can learn the Qur'an and we will become expert in the Sunna of Islam and the Shari'at."

15 This was the battle of Ayn Jalūt in Palestine where the Mongols suffered their 'first' major defeat. It had symbolic rather than military significance.

Page 38

They had planned that when Bunduqdār trusted them, on the day of the festival when Muslims come out and the people of Islam stand together in prayer, they would put hand to sword [**27b**] and strike out against the Muslims.

God Almighty wished that Bunduqdār be aware of this situation. Bunduqdār commanded that the Franks be treated well and until the day of the ʿĪd, he entrusted them to the care of a group of men. The Franks' designs were given away as two men took each of them by the shoulders. Bunduqdār's men realised that under their clothes all of them were wearing a coat of mail and a kaftan and underneath this they had short swords of Damascus steel which were seized. Thus the Franks were bound and carried to the place of the ʿĪd celebration, and there they were held.

Bunduqdār commanded his men to address the Franks thus, "First you must learn to stand in prayer. Afterwards we will instruct you in the sacrifice [*qorbān*]. When the Muslim community had performed their prayers, Bunduqdār ordered that they be cast in the manner of the sacrificial animal and their necks were slit with a knife in the same way as in the rites of the sacrifice.

When their clothes were removed, all of them were wearing fine coats of mail and fine kaftans. As soon as word of their finery reached the common people, they stripped them naked and from that time fear and dread that defies description entered into the hearts of the Franks and the Rūmiyeh. The few times that Hulegu sent an army to Syria, they [the Franks and the Rūmiyeh] would do nothing [*kārī nakardand*].

Page 39

After that, enmity arose between Hülegü and his kinsmen, and on account of their hostility Hülegü did not set out for Syria or Egypt but instead fought with Berke. A few times Hülegü went as far as Berke's lands,[16] in such a way that he passed a few *farsangs* beyond the gateway [*Darband*][17] to Saqsīn[18]

16 According to the *Yuan Si* Mongke had allotted Georgia to Berke.

17 Darband was in fact a port on the Caspian which traditionally held back the hellish forces of Gog and Magog, which also acted as a border between the Jochid Khanate and the Ilkhanate.

18 The location of Saqsīn is much debated. It was a mediaeval city that flourished from the eleventh to the thirteenth centuries. It was situated in the Volga Delta, or in the Lower Volga region, and was known in pre-Mongol times as Saksin-Bolgar, which in Mongol times became Sarai Batu.

and crossed the Terek River.[19] Finally, feeling secure, Hülegü's army struck camp among the houses and chattel that belonged to the army of [**28a**] Berke based in the province of Qipchaq. Berke's forces gathered from all directions and charged down upon Hülegü's forces.

[*The Caucasus had long been both highly prized and contentious as rich grazing land, strategically vital for defence, and a focus for trade routes. Mongke "allotted each prince of the blood (chu-wang) his own place . . . Berke (Pieh-erh-ko) with the territory of Georgia (Ch'u-erh-chihs)" Yuan Si, ch.3;*[20] *"To his eldest son, Tushi (Jochi), he (Chinggis Khan) gave the territory stretching from the regions of Qayaligh, and Khorazm to the remotest parts of Saqsin and Bulghar and as far in that direction as the hoof of Tartar horse had penetrated" Boyle, p. 42; Qazvīnī, vol.I, 31. The Caucasus had been claimed by many steppe nomads including the Saljuq Turks and later the Qipchaq Turks. Berke and his successors considered the Ilkhans usurpers of their ancestral lands.*[21]]

This army had become negligent and had allowed great calamity to fall upon them and in a rout, they came unto the seaport of Shābarān[22] [in Shirvan]. A great number of Hülegü's soldiers met death and destruction and Hülegü suffered greatly from this episode. He debated what kind of retaliation and retribution he might take for this affair, but he was incapacitated by black thoughts, and however much he tried to compose himself he relapsed into those dark thoughts once more.

[*In order to render this passage comprehensible, paraphrasing has been employed. Though Rashīd al-Dīn reports this setback and acknowledges Hulegu's "humiliating defeat," p. 1046, he concentrates on the many victories the Iranian forces enjoyed. Shīrāzī alone mentions that Hulegu seems to have suffered from periods of great depression.*]

At this time also, Hülegü had elevated the son of the Lesser [Kūchuk] Dawātdār, who they called Jalāl al-Dīn, to a grand position, and the khan imagined to himself that there was nobody dearer or more trustworthy in the whole of his territories or army.

This Jalāl declared that there were still a few thousand Qipchaq Turks in the caliph's territories that knew the roads and understood the customs

19 Rises in the Caucasus in N. Georgia, flows north through Ossetia and Chechnya, then drains into the Caspian in Daghestan.

20 Cited in Thomas Allsen, chapter 7, "Apportioned Lands under the Mongols", in Anatoly Khazanov and Andre Wink (eds.), *Nomads in the Sedentary World* (Curzon: Richmond, 2001), pp. 174–175.

21 See Peter Jackson, "Dissolution of the Mongol Empire", *Central Asiatic Journal*, Vol. 22 (Wiesbaden, 1978); George Lane, *Early Mongol Rule in 13th Century Iran* (London: Routledge, 2003), ch. 4, for more on this subject.

22 Situated on the coast of modern-day north Azerbaijan.

of that province [the Caucasus region]. If the king commanded, he would go and summon them so that "when you command us to return to the war against Berke, we may take them so that they may go ahead and provide us with intelligence."

Page 40

Forasmuch as Hülegü prior to this had seized Berke's soldiers and the persons who belonged to that quarter, and had killed some and imprisoned some, while others had fled, the grounds for this episode, the outbreak of hostilities with Berke, had become manifest in the year that Baghdad was taken [656/1258], when Balghāī, Tūtār and Tūlī [*Rashīd al-Dīn has Bulughā(n), Tūtār and Qulī, p. 1044*], who were Berke's close kinsmen, **[28b]** indeed his nephews, exercised authority in the realm [*dar mulk ḥukm mīkardand*]. If ever Hülegü nominated their forces for some task, they would openly say, "Since our troops do most of the work, let him, namely Hülegü, not threaten us." They harboured sentiments of this kind and from time to time they would pass remarks. Factious persons exaggerated the situation and reported things to the king, and for this reason he grew angry with them. It was also the case that Berke's *shaḥna*s and governors and his family held the choicest and best territories in Khorasan, ʿIraq, Azerbaijan, Arrān, and Georgia, and used to say, "These are our *injü*!" which means, their private property. And on every possible occasion factious persons would say things to aggravate the situation.

Page 41, events from the year 656/1256
[these events appear to break the chronological order]

Around that juncture, in the year 656/1258, Bālāqāī [*presumably this is the same prince, Balghāī, mentioned earlier*] died in the course of a feast [*ṭūy*]. After a short interval, Tūtār in turn was accused of sorcery and was sent to Berke for having done such a thing. Berke declared, "Since he is guilty, let Hülegü arrange it." Tūtār was brought back and Hülegü gave orders for his execution. This became the grounds for hostilities, so some years later Hülegü sent this Jalāl, the Dawātdār's son, to Baghdad for the reason that has previously been described, to bring back troops. The Ilkhan issued Jalāl al-Dīn with an edict: "Anyone from whom this Jalāl should deem prudent to ask, should furnish all horses, weapons, harnesses, provisions and funds; neither the governors of Baghdad nor any other living being should interfere in his activities, **[29a]** until he has accomplished what we have decreed."

[*Though only odd phrases appear verbatim, Rashīd al-Dīn pp. 1049–1051, again provides a more detailed account of events surrounding Jalāl al-Dīn's cooperation with Hulegu.*]

Page 42, year 662/1263

Jalāl went to Baghdad in the year 662/1263 and everybody recognised him. Those that spoke with him said that this is a man who is ready whether in the military or in other kinds of work. Jalāl al-Dīn sought them out and in secret said "The king has sent me to lead you into battle so that you can serve him in the front lines of the army. His intention is that you will die there, on the frontline, or you will make your name famous. If you are killed in that place, in your stead there are others who will continue the very same work."

"Now you all know me and whose son I am. I will not allow you to become sword fodder in the cause of an infidel. Although the king remains extremely favourable[23] towards me, my intention is that we declare our abandonment of this infidel state and fate. I will cast off the hand of these Mongols [*Moghūlān*] from myself and you."

Page 43

When he had spoken these words all were beguiled by his promises and an army was assembled. He immediately mounted before his troops and beat the drums and passed over the bridge to Baghdad to attack the Khafājeh Arabs, plundering a few oxen and camels. Jalāl al-Dīn took horses, weapons, pay, and complete provisions from Baghdad's treasury for the numbers of troops he had collected, and ordered that muster to decamp with their women, children, [**29b**] and everything else they possessed and again he beat the drum before crossing over the bridge.

He said "Let us take our women and children along with us to visit the holy shrines of the Imams, since after this my residence will be the province of Darband and those regions, and we will not have chance to return here. We men will go and take provisions, that is, plunder, for the road from the Khafājeh Arabs." And he went.

When he had crossed the Euphrates, Jalāl al-Dīn said to his own wives and the ordinary soldiers, "I have the idea of going to Syria and Egypt. Everyone who agrees, well and good, wonderful but otherwise those who so wish must turn back now from here." Even if in their hearts they did not want to go, they could not bring themselves, from fear, to say that they would return and so immediately adopting the manner of the enthusiast and the occupied (*por dākhteh*) they set out for Syria.

23 Iraj Afshar transcribes this word as ʻatāb meaning censure, displeasure which makes no sense. The ms is smudged and not clear but certainly ʻināyat – favour, bounty, is a possible transcription and makes more sense.

When this news reached the king's ears his anger was beyond description. For a long time, Hülegü wrung his hands, ground his teeth, and moaned that a little one should not tease him like this and such deceit was in excess of anything. He suffered a relapse of his ailments and sickness overcame him. He was seized by epilepsy and of all the kinds of doctors who attended him none were able to cope, for they did not know a cure.

[*Rashīd al-Dīn pp. 1049–51, includes this anecdote about the deceit of Jalāl al-Dīn and as can be seen from the underlined phrases indicating verbatim descriptions, the two accounts must share a common source. However, significantly Rashīd al-Dīn excludes all mention of Hulegu's seemingly pathological depression and the full extent of his reaction to Jalāl al-Dīn's treachery. Ḥamdallah Mustawfī Qazvīnī refers to Hulegu's depression when he describes the Shah's death: then Hulegu also became disturbed at heart. Those doctors who were near him could see no remedy from that severe pain, and no one could find a cure for the pain in his soul. Ward tr., p. 210; ms 633a.*]

Page 44, year 663 (1264/65)

In Rabī' al-Akhar in the year 663/January 1265, on the border of Maragheh on the banks of the river that they call the Jaghātū, Hülegü passed away. He had 13 sons.

Meanwhile, his oldest son, Abaqa, was in Khorasan and Yoshmut was on the border of Shirwan [**30a**] and Darband, so someone was sent to summon them. Neither arrived while Hülegü lived.

Yoshmut arrived on the third day after his father's death and he resided at court two days for consultation concerning official affairs and then returned to his own place.

Abaqa arrived after a few days from the province of Sitārbāḍ and Gorgān and he also did not stay in Hülegü's ordu, returning early to his own place.

Dokuz [Ṭoghūz] Khatun, who had been the wife of Tolui Khan, also died in that week. She had enjoyed great authority and her orders were always executed.

[*Though Hulegu had inherited Dokuz Khatun from his father, Tolui Khan, and she bore him no children, she was considered his primary wife and had great influence over him. Mongke Khan had instructed his brother to "consult Dokuz Khatun on all matters" (RaD, p. 977) when he dispatched him on his epic march to the West.*]

After a short time, five or six months later, they convened a quriltai [*qūrīltāī*][24] and Abaqa was placed on the throne.

24 Convocation, jamboree, council meeting of Mongol elite to decide on matters of state.

Page 45

He cared greatly for the troops . . . a period of 17 years . . . these regions that have been mentioned and his father had captured . . . machination repeatedly? . . . in such a way that he did no harm to . . . that in ruins . . . they did, they took, and they killed and in . . . before they came . . . done sufficiently . . . they were with the Mongol and great and difficult work that he . . . because Hülegü's war . . . he with Mongol when Berke . . . that with difficult . . .

[*This page is incomprehensible and even Īraj Afshār abandoned the attempt to transcribe the words from the original where they are scrawled into the margins of the page.*]

Page 46, year 667/1258–59

In the year 667, the senior wife of Hülegü, Qutui Khatun [*Qūtūī, and other similar spellings*], because of the disorder in that province, arrived from Turkestan. Her two elder sons, Takeshī[n][25] and Tekūdār (later Sultan Ahmad), who had wives and children, accompanied her.

Abaqa had great respect for them and gave them a great many possessions and land. His own concubine named Ārqān was from the house of Qutui (Qūtī) Khatun. She had come with Hülegü from that place, from Qutui's ordu, and whatever was Qutui Khatun's share, this Ārqān used to appropriate it. At the time of the death of Hülegü, she struck herself with a knife and killed herself. When Qūtī Khatun came to her home, it so happened that her house was richly decorated with a variety of items.

[*This sparse account is explained more clearly in Rashīd al-Dīn pp. 1064–65. Qutui had been abandoned, feared lost, in hostile Turkestan and Arqān had assumed her position at court. With Qutui's reappearance, she presumably feared punishment and took her own life though this detail is unique to Shīrāzī's text. As well as her own two sons, she cared for Jushkab (Jūshkāb) and Kingshü, the sons of her brother-in-law, Jomqur who had died en route.*]

Abaqa arrived from the province of Diyarbakr and Miyāfārqīn and he awarded Qutui Khatun a few provinces, from which each year she accrued about 100,000 *Khalīftī* dinar, and that income was squandered foolishly. [**30b**]

Even though Abaqa would continually lavish them with gifts, attention, provisions, flocks, and herds, they [Qutui's party] resented his position as sovereign.

25 This should be Takshin; Prince Takshī was the son of Böchök, half-brother of Hulegu.

Page 47

A short while later Yoshmut, whose summer domicile was in Georgia, and in winter resided at the confines of Ganjeh and Barda^{c}a, died. After him, Tekshī[n] died.

Yoshmut had a brother, a very brave and judicious man who used to represent Abaqa in Khorasan. He also died.

Abaqa Khan allowed every country and region that he had given to his brothers to pass on to their offspring and he made no difficulty for any of them.

Page 48, year 675 (1276/77)

In the year 675, Bunduqdār of Syria took an army to Rum; and in that place, there were two great amirs with a great army. These special Mongols were called Tūqū (Tughu Bitigchi) bin Elkāī and Tūdavān (Tödä'ün) bin Sodūn.[26]

Rukn al-Dīn Bunduqdār (d. 1277) engaged them in battle in Ābolestān of Rum. He destroyed that army, killed those two amirs, and took up his residence for a short time at Caesarea in Rum, in anticipation of what Mo^{c}īn al-Dīn Parvana,[27] who was lord of Rum, had perchance promised him. "If you come, I will give you the crown of Rum." The Parvāna feared that the Mongols would act treacherously towards him.

Because Rukn al-Dīn Bunduqdār remained in Caesarea [*Qīṡeriyeh*] for close to a week and he did not allow or give permission for his own army to plunder, sustaining that army became difficult. The Parvāna did not present himself before him [**31a**] and had retreated to a castle and remained there. Bunduqdār withdrew from Rum towards Syria.

When news reached Abaqa, he set out in person for Rum with a vast army. But by the time he was on the move, Bunduqdār had gone, so Abaqa returned.

26 These were Elgäi Noyan's son and Suqunjaq Noyan's brother.

27 Mu'īn al-Dīn Sulaiman Parvāna, r.1261–77; In 1277, Baybars entered the Seljuk sultanate and on 18 March, overcame the Mongol army in Elbistan, while the Pervāneh, who was in command of the Saljuq forces expected by both Baybars and the Mongols, took flight to Tokat along with the young sultan. Baybars made a triumphal entry into Kayseri on 23 April and then returned to Syria. At the news of his troops' defeat, Abaqa hastened to Anatolia (July 1277) and punished the Saljuqi Turks, sources citing massacres of tens of thousands of people. Deeming him responsible for Baybars's foray into Anatolia, Abaqa also had Pervāneh killed, eaten according to Hetoum, on 2 August 1277.

Page 49, to Syria by way of Diyarbakir

The next year Abaqa set out for Syria. He himself went to Raḥbeh in Syria, and he sent his brother Möngke Temur (1256–82), the son of Uljayi [Ūljā] Khatun, to whom he had given command of the army, Möngke Temur[28] set off and he confronted a Syrian army on the borders of Homs and Hama. By this time, Bunduqdār had died, and the king and commander of that country was called Alfī,[29] a Qipchaq Turk who had also been a slave of the sultans of Syria, namely the family of Salāh al-Dīn. They battled, and the army of Prince Möngke Temur was severely routed and forced to retreat.

Abaqa Khan was extremely pained from this outcome and he would not turn his face to his brother. He said that it was clear that the following year he would go himself to see what could be done. He spent the winter in Baghdad.

They [had] seized ʻAlā' al-Dīn, the Ṣāḥib Dīvān, and mulcted him, plundering all his palaces and houses and placing a double yoke on his neck. The foundation for this calamity had been laid one year previously by Majd al-Mulk Yazdī. He had thrust himself into Abaqa's service, after 40 or 50 persons, all scribes and men of distinction, had come forward to attack and harass the ṣāḥib-dīwāns, ʿAlā' al-Dīn Aṭā Malik and Shams al-Dīn Muḥammad; and there were many grandees of whom the people calculated **[31b]** that they would one day work for the dismissal of the ṣāḥibs. However, not a soul suspected that behind such an affair lay a hand like that of Majd al-Mulk [Yazdī].[30]

Page 50, year 679/1280–81

Meanwhile Majd al-Mulk in the season of spring of the year 679/1281 in Sharūyāz, in between Abhar and Zangān at the Muslim Fort, presented himself before Abaqa in the hot baths of the slaughterhouse and explained this matter to him. Prior to this situation arising, Abaqa had grown estranged from the [Juwaynī] brothers and sought a pretext to act against them.

When Majd al-Mulk spoke about the state of the court finances, they [the Juwaynīs] became afraid and very uncomfortable. But Shams al-Dīn bore up as had been his custom in the past and he was not made to appear.

28 See Rashīd al-Dīn, p. 969; youngest brother of Abaqa; he married Abish Khatun of Shiraz.

29 al-Malik al-Manṣūr Saif ad-Dīn Qalā'ūn al-Alfi as-Ṣālihī an-Najmī al-ʿAlā'ī, r.1279–90; sold for 1000 dinars in 1240s into household of Sultan al-Kamīl.

30 Rashīd al-Dīn recounts this episode in far greater detail, pp. 1110–1117; 1126–1128; see George Lane and Michal Biran on the Juwayni brothers in Encyclopedia Iranica.

'Alā' al-Dīn was summoned from Baghdad, and when he arrived in Siah Kuh [Siyāh Kūh],[31] they demanded that the property of his that he had taken from the king must be returned. Majd al-Dīn ibn Athīr presided in front of him probing whether he had acquired the property from this or that person or place.

Shams al-Dīn had told his brother not to renounce his principles [*hīch bāb ankār makon*] unless they tortured him and reminded him that wealth is not worth lost honour. 'Alā' al-Dīn was put in a headlock so that he would surrender 300 tūmān of gold to them.

Page 51

When they returned to Maragheh from Siah Kuh, Abaqa, with all of his amirs and the pillars of the government and many of the royal ladies, was in the Butkhāneh [*Buddhist temple*].

That day Abaqa commanded that they write a royal proclamation on behalf of Majd al-Mulk to be read before the assembled people. Everyone was in agreement that Mongol kings had never before granted anyone such a *yarlīgh*.

When they proclaimed the *yarlīgh*, Abaqa told Majd al-Mulk that he must pay great attention to affairs of state, the administration, the treasury, and the livestock [**34a**] and all that is his. "Watch closely everything your deputies do and keep guard on yourself and never be separated from me. Anyone who is an enemy to you is an enemy to me. Those that are friends with you are friends of mine. Henceforth, if anyone makes an attack on you, I will be with you."

Because Abaqa had issued such an extreme mark of favour, the whole network of amirs and notables was disrupted, and Majd al-Mulk sent deputies to all the notables, all the tax districts and provinces, everywhere from within Rum to the end of Khorasan and from the deserts of Arabia until the borders of Saqsīn.[32] He raised an edifice the likes of which nobody had ever seen. In the space of seven or eight months a person who had been of no account anywhere now managed a business of such great complexity. Everybody was amazed.

When they returned from Maragheh to Baghdad, as has been mentioned, they confiscated lands from the minister ʿAlā' al-Dīn.

31 This had been the site of Abaqa's summer pastures. It was a mountain overlooking the town of Kalandar in Azerbaijan, near the source of the Jaghatu River.

32 Volga delta, with the capital in Sarai Batu.

Page 52, year 680 [1281/82]

At the end of winter Abaqa went to Hamadan. He had a very great love of wine and he would drink excessively. He drank in Bahrāmshāh's house[33] until night; and in the middle of the night, he had a need to go outside, and from on top of the lavatory he fell off and died. It was such that a little life remained in his body so they carried him into the house. He [died] on the way.

This was on 20th Ḍu al-Ḥijja 680 (1st April 1282). Abaqa's body was taken to the burial site of his father and of some of his brothers, on the island that is known as Shahiyeh in the centre of Azerbaijan near Dehkhwārqān.

[*Shāhī Island, now called Islami Island (Jezīra-ye Islāmī), has now merged with the mainland and houses the main ferry link connecting the two sides of Urumiya Lake and the main road between Tabriz and Urumiya. Though evidence has been found of burial sites, tomb robbers long ago despoiled the treasures left by Hulegu and his successors.*]

Page 53

In consultation with all of the princes, that is Abaqa's brothers and his sons, they seated Prince Tegüdar, whom they call **[34b]** Sultan Ahmad, on the royal throne on 26th Moharram 681 (6th May 1282).

Page 54, year 682 (1283/84)

In the year 682/1283–84 Sultan Ahmad sent his brother, known as Qonghartai [*Qonghartāī*], to rule Rum. The Sultan appointed Qonghartai the commander of the army which accompanied him to Anatolia (Rum). This army enabled him to deal with the rebels and to protect Rum from the Syrian army.

Qonghartai arrived in Rum with his army and behaved mercilessly towards people who were very loyal (*īl*), cooperative, and contributive (*qalān-bīsh*), massacring and enslaving them and taking a great many prisoners.

[*This implied criticism of Qonghartai is not found in Rashīd al-Dīn who claims that 4th Rabīᶜ II 681 (12th July 1282), Ahmad rewarded his brother with a wife, Toqiyatai Khatun, before sending him off to Anatolia, p. 1129.*]

As the news reached Sultan Ahmad's ears, he summoned Qonghartai back. Qonghartai had plotted with Prince Arghun (*Oghul*[34]), the eldest son of Abaqa, to betray Sultan Ahmad.

33 This reference remains obscure.

34 'Son' in Turkish, used as a title for sons of the royal family, with royal blood, and it follows the given name hence Arghun Oghul. Translated by 'Prince'.

As soon as Sultan Ahmad found out about this collusion, he acted pre-emptively, and on 28th Shawāl/18th January 1284 in Arran, he had Qong-hartai arrested and annihilated.[35]

[*The reasons behind Ahmad's execution of Qonghartai differ in Shīrāzī's account from that in Rashīd al-Dīn where there is a perfunctory reference to a loss of trust between the two and a suspicion of a plot between Arghun and his uncle, p. 1133. Shīrāzī makes no mention of Shaykh 'Abdul-Rahman or the infamous Ishan Mangali, a hashish-smoking qalandar, both reputedly influential in Ahmad's inner court.*[36]]

Ahmad also executed the two other amirs, Kūckak and Sādī [Shadai Aqtachi], who were in agreement with Qonghartai, and got busy sorting out the other rebels.

* * *

Page 55

The reason for mentioning this account was that one day Qonghartai came to the ordu, and in the presence of Ahmad and Qutui Khatun and all the amirs, said: "Tomorrow when Ahmad and Arghun do battle, my retainers and I will withdraw to a private place and we will not take part in the fight."

After that he retired to his winter quarters. The gossip mongers and slanderers took the opportunity to whisper poisoned words to Ahmad and claimed, "Qonghartai has shared your women in the same way that your own kids and amirs have" and the like.

Meanwhile **[36a]** Kuchak came snooping all around Ahmad's ordu, ten days before Qonghartai. People told Ahmad that Kuchak had come spying and that he had come to gather intelligence about what was happening in the ordu in order to inform Qonghartai.

Because Ahmad's ears had been filled with such ideas, he ordered that his men should seize Qonghartai, a command which they carried out at midday of Wednesday 28th Shawāl 682 (19th January 1284) and that same night Qonghartai's back was broken. This was in accordance with the precepts of Chinggis Khan, who had said that the back of whosoever plots against the kingdom should be broken.

35 Literally 'nothinged' *nīst gardānīd.*

36 On Ishan Manglali see Lane, 2003, pp. 245–248; and Judith Pfeiffer, "Ahmad's Second Letter . . . ", in Judith Pfeiffer and Sholeh A. Quinn (eds.), *History and Historiography of Post-Mongol Central Asia and the Middle East: Studies in Honour of John E. Woods* (Weisbaden: Harrassowitz, 2006), pp. 167–202.

Afterwards they interrogated Kuchak and asked him what Qonghartai and Arghun had conspired to do. He said he did not know. They beat him with a cane a hundred times but still he did not confess.

When this was reported to Ahmad, he said: "Kuchak is an old man, a deceiver and a bastard and never tells the truth. Kill him and his son."

Page 56

Kuchak and his son were both said to be *gakamashī*. This is a term used among the Mongols when they want to kill someone. If the person says "Kākū", which is the name of a bird, he will not be killed. It is well known among Mongols that should they put that person to death, the killer will be cursed. So Ahmad ordered that they should execute Kuchak but that his son should be spared.

For the next seven days after Qonghartai's killing, an armed force formed a *nerge* standing guard around the ordu. And because the reason for these killings was the victims' friendship with Arghun, it was realised that Arghun was going to retaliate and it was thought best to muster the troops and embark on war against Arghun.

First to arrive was Tubat who was the nephew of Ahmad and the son of Tabshīn, with Prince Baṡar (Yasar), who was also of royal birth.[37]

Alinaq and Māzūq and Shāżī (Shadai), the son of Suqunjaq, and Āchū Sokarchī with eight thousand riders rode out from the region of Mansuriya in Arran. **[36b]**

* * *

On 9th Dhu'l-Qa'dah 682 (29th January 1284), after three days,[38] there was severe snow and due to the difficulty of the road, Tubat and Baṡar (Yasar), who were riding alongside Alinaq, fell behind; and they sent an envoy ahead to announce this delay. Ahmad commented on how slowly they were moving.

Alinaq, along with 200 men, reached the neighbourhood of Ray and attacked a group of people who were part of Arghun's court, robbed them, and then returned to Qazvin with his followers.

Page 57, year 683/1283–84

[*Rashīd al-Dīn mentions in an entry for Thursday, 18th Muharram, 683 (6th April 1284) that Ahmad married Tödäi Khatun who though she remained close to him later married Arghun who honoured her greatly, placing a boqtaq on her head (pp. 1056,1134).]*

37 Brother of the Chaghadaid prince, Baraq.

38 Rashīd al-Dīn has 'Alīnāq et al. riding out on the 9*th*, and the snow starting on the 12th.

When Arghun heard the news, he mobilised with six thousand riders and made Yula Temur [*Yūlā Tāmūr and Yūlā Timūr*][39] the commander of the army.

[*Rashīd al-Dīn claims that Arghun sent Yūlā/Ulai Temūr as his vanguard with Emgächin Noyan close behind him.*]

Hulechu was Tubat and Alinaq's [*ᶜAlīnāq*] *gäjigä* (*kachakeh*),[40] namely the army that is behind the advance guard, and Ṭījū and Tekanā followed with ten thousand riders. In the rear came Ahmad, who left Pilsuvar [*Bīlsavār*],[41] which is in Mughan, on Wednesday 8th Safar 683 (26th April 1284) with eight *tūmān* of troops – a *tūmān* is ten thousand.

On Monday 13th Safar (1st May 1284) an envoy from Tubat arrived to announce that Arghun's army had been sighted [in Talaqan[42]].

The next day, another envoy arrived and brought the same news. From the neighbourhood of Ardabil, Ahmad sent Qurumshi, the son of Alinaq, to his father with the message that "If you are greater in number, then fight; and if they are more then you, wait for us to arrive."

Ahmad then left behind his heavy baggage (*ughruq*), and on the day of Saturday 18th Safar (6th May 1284)[43] he departed in haste from Ardabil with the army, and every day he covered two stages.

Thursday 16th Safar (4th May 1284), after midday, under the influence of the star sign, Virgo, Arghun clashed until sunset with Tubat and Alinaq in Jamālābād near Qazvin, which the Mongols call Āq Khwājeh, and some groups from both armies fled the battlefield.

[*This is the famous battle where the Sufi poet, ᶜAlā al-Dawlah Simnānī (1261–13336) experienced his transformative noetic mystic vision which caused him to leave Arghun Khan's service for the contemplative life. Simnānī remained in a mystic state throughout the battle and into the next day.*][44]

Page 58

Arghun [**33a**] slept one night on the battlefield while some of his people from the village of Jamālābād, located about ten *farsangs* from the battle, were forced to flee from Tubat's army.

39 Yūlā Tāmūr's son, Baqā'ī, was one of Mustawfī's informants. He is called Ulai Temür in Rashīd al-Dīn.

40 Rearguard or reserve troops, see Rashīd al-Dīn, pp. 171, 883 and entries in Doefer Turkish-Mongol dictionary, ∞357.

41 A town in the province of Arran.

42 This same story appears in Rashīd al-Dīn almost verbatim on p. 1136.

43 Wheeler Thackston questions the accuracy of this date in his translation of Rashīd al-Dīn, p. 392, n.2.

44 For a fuller account of this incident and further references and context, see Jamal J. Elias, *The Throne Carrier of God: The Life and Thought of ᶜAlā al-Dawlah Simnānī* (Albany: State University of New York Press, 1995), pp. 18–21.

[*Rashīd al-Dīn explains the involved action behind these brief words. While Arghun's army won on the battlefield, elements of the defeated army attacked his baggage train, infuriating the prince, all the more so because he was unable to take action against these armed elements (pp. 1136–37).*]

On Monday 20th Safar (8th May 1284) Tubat's envoy reached Ahmad's camp and he brought glad tidings that "We have fought Arghun and he has fled and we have taken many prisoners from his army. The rearguard (*gäjigä* / *kachakeh*) never caught up with us" [pp. 1137–38]. Ahmad was angry because he knew about this setback (*tawaquf*) from Tekanā (Totqavul).[45] That day they celebrated and made merry.

The next day, Ahmad reached Zangān, and on Thursday 23rd Safar (11th May 1284) he joined Tubat in Sharviyāz and that day they celebrated and made merry.

The next day, prince Huleju[46] was dispatched with a tūmān (10,000) of troops in the direction of Ray, while Ahmad and his commanders positioned themselves in Sharviyāz for two days.

On Monday 27th Safar (15th May) news arrived that Prince Gaykhatu [*Geikhātū*] had set out from the vicinity of Hamadan on the pretext of hunting and fled to Khorasan with a few of his people.

[*This entry is missing from Rashīd al-Dīn.*]

The next day (Tuesday, 16th May) Ahmad left his wife, Armini [*Armanī*] Khatun, in Sharviyāz and set off. On the same day Jushkab [*Jūshkāb*][47] arrived from the direction of Baghdad.

The next day (29th Safar/17th May) Ahmad reached Āq Khwājeh [*near Qazvin*], which was the site of the battle of Jamālābād.

The next day they reached Qazvin and reviewed the army. That day Lagzi [*Lakzī*],[48] the son of Arghun Aqa [*Arghūn Āghā*], [*the term āghā is an honorific title for a civilian or military officer, but the minister Arghun Aqa's name and title are usually spelt this way in secondary sources*] together with Ordu Buqa son of Nawruz, arrived from Arghun's presence. They delivered their khan's apologies, saying: "How can I draw a sword in my Āghā's face? It was never in my mind. But when Alinaq attacked me and plundered, *I*

45 Highway patrol.

46 Twelfth son of Hulegu, son of concubine in Dokuz Khatun's ordu.

47 Son of Jumqur, son of Hulegu. He arrived in Iran with Qutui Khatun just after Hulegu's death. Ahmad had assigned him duties in Baghdad.

48 Lagzi Gürägän, son of the former governor of Iran (1243–55), the Oiyat Amir Arghun Aqa [d.1278]. Lagzi married Hulegu's seventh daughter, Baba. His brother Nawruz [d.1297] married Abaqa's daughter, Toghanchuq, and was instrumental in the conversion of Ghazan Khan [r.1295–1304] to Islam.

came to see if he had arrayed his army [**33b**] against me. It was necessary for me to do battle."

Page 59

Later that night Lagzi secretly separated from Ordu Buqa, and together they pledged allegiance, and [promised that] Lagzi would remain on the side of Ahmad and that he would keep them informed of all developments in Arghun's camp.

[*No mention of this in Rashīd al-Dīn who presents Arghun's envoys presenting a united front and Ahmad refusing to listen to any talk of compromise, "Ahmad refused to listen" p. 1138. The following entry is not found in Rashīd al-Dīn.*]

* * *

On Sunday 4th of Rabīᶜ al-Aval (21st May 1284), Ahmad sent Arghun's messengers back. Following them on Monday 5th Rabīᶜ al-Aval (22nd May 1284), he sent Tuq Temūr, the son of Abdallah Āghā (general of Abaqa) and Temur to be there when Arghun should ask his sons to come and sit down together, saying such and such and suggest that they all sort things out. "And if Arghun cannot come, let him send Yula Temur and [*the Grand Amir*] Shishi Bakhshi [*Shīshī Bakhshī*] and Qadān and his sons." Behind these emissaries, Ahmad moved forward with the army.

On Wednesday 14th Rabīᶜ al-Aval (31st May 1284), ambassadors returned and they brought the princes, Ghazan [*Qazān*] (r.1295–1304) the son of Arghun Khan, and Prince Omar the son of [Ahmad] Tegudar Yaghī, and the amirs Noghai Yarghuchi [*Nuqāī Yarghūchī*],[49] Shishi Bakhshi [*Shīshī Bakhshī*], and Qadān.[50]

These amirs suggested that the king, Ahmad, withdraw from that locality so that Arghun himself would be prepared to come, "For at this moment the king is angry and he, Arghun, is afraid." Ahmad did not listen and did not retreat, despite the fact that the amirs considered it advisable that he should withdraw. Though his army had been weakened, whenever anyone mentioned this to Ahmad he would reply that he would advance. "Let anyone who wishes come with me; if they do not, let them withdraw."

49 Noghai Yarghuchi is of the Baya'ut tribe, and he was connected through marriage with the royal family. As a yarghuchi, a judge, he presided over disputes and rifts among the ruling classes.

50 It is not clear who this amir is. Qadan, Guyuk's brother, was serving with Qubilai; Shishi Bakhshi was associated with Sönitäi Noyan and his sons, including Emgächin, and the infamous and ambitious Ṫaghājār [Taghachar] Noyan.

Page 60

The next day, 16th Rabīᶜ al-Aval (2nd June), Ahmad sent back Arghun's amirs and the following day, Saturday (17th Rabīᶜ al-Aval/3rd June), he arrived in Girdeh Kuh [*also written Girdkuh; Rashīd al-Dīn claims Ribat-i-Akhari, p. 1139*], and in that place he took recreation and promenade. [**35a**] It was from there that Ahmad dispatched the sons of prince Taghai Temur [*Ṭaghā Timūr*], who was a brother of Ahmad, and Sogai [*Sūkā*], son of prince Yoshmut; and from among the amirs he sent Buqa Āghā[51] and Doladāī Yarghuchi. Ahmad told Buqa Āghā that he must bring back Arghun and if he would not come, he should bring back Gaykhatu [r.1291–95] together with the amirs whom Ahmad had himself sent back. Buqa Āghā set off and found Arghun in Khuchān.

Ahmad arrived in Damghan with the army on Sunday (18th Rabīᶜ al-Aval/4th June) and the town was pillaged. Ahmad did not forbid this plundering of Damghan for the reason that his army became debilitated.

[*Rashīd al-Dīn emphasises pillage and torture in Damghan, p. 1139.*]

And when they arrived at Kharraqān, Bulghān, who was the *shaḥna* of Shiraz, together with Jurghudāī, who was an amir of a thousand, came to pay homage to Ahmad and they declared themselves *īl*.

The next day, 23rd Rabī' I (9th June), Ahmad sent Alinaq from Kharraqān to Menkalī with Ṫuṫāq, an amir of a thousand, Qara Buqa, the son of Altajū, and three thousand men. The next day, Ahmad went.

Tuesday 27th Rabīᶜ I, (13th June 1284) the envoy Buqa Āghā arrived in order to collect Prince Gaykhatu.

[*On 28th Rabī' I, (13th June 1284) Rashīd claims that Ahmad "dismounted in Kalpus." p. 1139.*]

After a day or so, the final day of Rabīᶜ I, Buqa Āghā arrived, bringing Prince Gaykhatu with him. Ahmad asked Buqa Āghā, "Why didn't you bring back any of the amirs who had returned earlier?" Buqa Āghā said: "I didn't understand that the pādeshāh wanted them." It was for this reason that Ahmad was angry with Buqa Āghā.

After that Ahmad left Gaykhatu with Tutāī Khatun[52] in Kalpush [*Kalehpūsh*] near Jājaram. From that place, he mustered the army and set off for Quchan (Khūchān), and they did not take one woman with them.

51 Buqa son of the Jalayir Ögöläi Qorchi, executed 1289 after a prestigious career as vizier then Chingsang under Arghun. He first served under Abaqa with his brother Aruq. Many believe that Buqa was the real power behind Arghun's throne and that he was planning a coup against the king when he was finally arrested.

52 A much sought-after lady, who began life as a concubine of Abaqa's.

Page 61

As soon as Arghun [**35b**] heard that Ahmad was coming, he retraced his steps. When Ahmad arrived in Quchan (Khūchān/Khabūshān) (9th Rabīᶜ II/25th June), his troops devastated that city. Then after they passed from that place, Arghun with about 100 people made for Kalat [*Kolāteh*] Kuh castle situated in Astav near Tus.

[*Rashīd al-Dīn adds that Bulaghan Khatun, wife of Abaqa Khan was at the castle to greet him, p. 1140.*]

Meanwhile Lagzi, who had pledged himself to Ahmad, attacked and pillaged the house of Arghun's wife, Qutlugh Khatun. In the same way, Arghun, when he had first started fighting Alinaq, had sent someone to the Qara'unas[53] and they had flocked to his, Arghun's support. Then when they heard that Arghun had been defeated, they turned around and every town that lay in their path, they attacked and pillaged.

When Ahmad had passed through the city of Quchan, Lagzi's wife, Baba, who was the sister of Abaqa Khan, came to offer homage to Ahmad. It was also on that day that there was rejoicing when Ahmad was informed that Arghun had fled to Kalat [*Kolāteh*] Kuh castle. Alinaq and his retainers with a small army went in pursuit of Arghun in order to prevent him leaving the castle.

The Qara'unas had now become estranged from Arghun, and for this reason it was not possible to escape in that direction, so it was necessary to come out on the same side from which he had entered the fortress.

Alinaq with his army, presuming that Arghun would come to fight, made preparation for war.

Page 62

Arghun sent Altāī to Alinaq's lines saying: "I am coming to see Ahmad." After that, with Bulaghan [*Bulaghān*] Khatun and other royal ladies, Arghun presented himself before Ahmad in the meadow [**37a**] of Rādkān (rāyekān) on Thursday 13th Rabīᶜ al-Akhar [*text has 'al-Aval' erroneously*] (29th June 30th May 1284).

On the day that Arghun arrived, because Ahmad ascribed a secret motive to his commanders who used to speak about Arghun in such a way that it

53 The Qara'unas are also called the Negudaris. Originally formed under Sali Noyan in the 1250s to protect the eastern border against the Delhi Sultanate, they later fell under the sway of fleeing Jochid troops, loyal to the Golden Horde. They remained renegade loosely allied with the Chaghadaid khans in later decades based in Khorasan. In 1279 Abaqa brought them to submission and some were rewarded with lands in the west.

would lead to ill-will, he faced all the top amirs and demanded of them, "Now, whose claim was right?" No one could say anything.

Buqa Āghā said happily, "My Happy King, your words were right."

He said, "Since my words were right, tomorrow we will go before 'Ātū'," that is, his mother Qutui Khatun. "Let everyone prepare their own speeches." All the amirs, and especially Buqa Āghā, feared these words.

On Friday, 14th of the month (Rabīᶜ II, 30th June), Ahmad struck camp and then returned two *farsangs*. Then on Saturday, the rest decamped since that day at Sar-cheshma, Bulaghan Khatun was holding a feast for Ahmad. In the middle of that feast Alinaq, Ṫutāq, and Qarā Buqa said to each other in drunkenness that as long as Ahmad had not killed those princes, his kingship would not be secure.

The night of Sunday, 16th of the month (Rabīᶜ II/2nd July), Ahmad entrusted Arghun to the army charging them with guarding him while Ahmad himself, with 200 horsemen, went to Kalpush, the place where Tutāī Khatun and Gaykhatu were ensconced, since Ahmad had previously sent Gaykhatu to that place.

When Ahmad had gone, Buqa Āghā sent someone to his older brother, Aruq [*Ārukh*] Āghā saying, "Ahmad has plans for us. What is to be done?" Aruq Āghā was with Jushkab [*Jūshkāb*].

Aruq said that Qaramush (Qurumshi), the son of Hindu Āghar (Hinduqur),[54] had come and given them the news that during Bulaghan Khatun's feast, Alinaq and others had also had just such a conversation. The brothers, Buqa Āghā and Aruq Āghā, met up with each other and they involved Jushkab in their plans.

Page 63

They befriended Tekanā[55] who had also had suspicions regarding Ahmad, [**37b**] and because Tekanā was with Huleju, they said that they would be prepared to give the crown to Huleju.

In short, all the amirs and princes were in agreement and they were all enjoying the feast during which they encouraged Alinaq to drink wine. Alinaq insisted that since that night it was his watch [*gäzik*] and he had to guard Arghun, he could not drink.

Jushkab said that he would guard Arghun on his behalf. Alinaq trusted him. They got Alinaq drunk and that same night they got Arghun mounted on a horse with Buqa Āghā. Arghun rode direct to the house of Alinaq.

54 Rashīd al-Dīn seems to suggest that this is Qurumshi Kuregan, son of Alinaq.

55 This is Amir Tägänä Totqavul, general under Abaqa.

And that very night which was the night of Monday, 17th Rabīᶜ II (3rd July), they made an end of Alinaq and they also killed Ṫuṫāq.[56]

Also that night, someone was sent to Huleju and Tekanā to say: "We have killed Alinaq and Ṫuṫāq. You must kill Baṡar Oghul and Abukān." Because Huleju hated Prince Baṡar (Yasar) but liked Abukān, they killed Prince Baṡar with a bowstring and preserved the latter, Abukān.

[*See Rashīd al-Dīn pp. 1142–44 for a more detailed version, with some differences.*]

On the day of Tuesday 18th Rabī' II (4th July 1284), someone from Ṫuṫāq's unit (*hazara* or *mingghan*, 1000 soldiers) was near Kūrūī, which was a dependency of Isfarāyīn. At midday, he reached Ahmad and told him that Ṫuṫāq had been killed and there was alarm within the army. The Amir, Aq Buqa,[57] took him to address Ahmad and the soldier explained the situation. They consulted astronomers and inquired about their own circumstances. After that, Ahmad retreated and settled near Isfarāyīn.

The next day, a messenger arrived from Māzuq Āghā to inform Ahmad that his enemies had killed all his supporters and that they were now all united. "If you can, get yourself out."

Page 64

The day of Wednesday 19th Rabīᶜ II (5th July 1284), Ahmad fled from the vicinity of Isfarāyīn in the direction of Kalpush. Halfway there at Jājarm, Khwājeh, the sāḥib dīwān (Shams al-Dīn Juwaynī) came and informed Ahmad: "We have no animals. If Ahmad permits, I will go to Gūyān (Juwayn) **[38a]** in order to bring a dromedary into service for the desert road to Yazd." Ahmad declared, "Let it be so!" The khwājeh[58] (Shams al-Dīn Juwaynī[59]) separated from Ahmad at that very place, Jājarm, and they were never to meet again. May God have mercy upon them.

[*This encounter is not mentioned in Rashīd al-Dīn at all though he does mention the Khwājeh's journey by camel to Yazd, p. 1156. Rashīd al-Dīn does suggest that Ahmad managed to have some moments of intimacy at this time with Tödäi Khatun when he reached Kalpush.*]

56 Taitaq son of Qubai Noyan was Abaqa Khan's *kükältash*, and Ahmad's amir-ordu. In fact he was not killed and was allowed to escape after his capture.

57 Tenth son of one of Hulegu's chief generals, the Jalayir Elgäi Noyan, excelled under Gaykhatu, killed by Baidu.

58 Khwāja/khwajeh can be translated as lord; it is an honorary title awarded respected notables, great merchants, and respected clerics.

59 Without Sultan Ahmad's support, the Juwaynī brothers had little defence against their powerful enemies among whom was Arghun Khan and both were dead within a short time of Ahmad's demise.

When Ahmad arrived at Armini Khatun's ordu in Shariviyār, where Suqunjaq Āghā was waiting, he commanded that the house of Buqa Āghā be plundered.

It was in that region that Ahmad was told that Yula Temur had been captured, "What must be done with him?" He demanded, "Don't you know what must be done? He and his followers must be executed according to the yasa. Despite such crimes as he has committed he came to me and I said to him, go to the ordu of Armini (Khatun) and wait until I come, and he fled." In short, Yula Temur and his dependents were killed.

[*Rashīd al-Dīn places this episode after Ahmad's flight from Isfarāyīn on 19th Rabī 5th July, encountering Yula Temur travelling from Mazanderan. After killing them, Ahmad's party turns towards Qumis and Persia. p. 1145*]

Ahmad came to Sarāū (Sarāb) to the ordu of Qutui Khatun, where he was joined by about two thousand persons. He wanted to disappear [*khwāst keh az gūsheh'ī beh dar ravad*]. Sakat (Shiktür Noyan)[60] Āghā and Qarā Noqāī, a son of Prince Yoshmut, said that if he left they would not be able to answer to the princes, amirs, and Arghun. They kept him under observation.

[*This episode is not recorded by Rashīd al-Dīn.*]

When this large group of rebels reached Kharraqān, they formed an assembly to declare who should be the king. They wanted to know when exactly Ahmad had fled. First they had to decide his fate.

Then Charīk the Mongol was sent with Ṫulāī Yarghūchī to track Ahmad down and behind them went Arghun and Buqa Āghā, and following them, the princes Hulaju and Gaykhatu [r.1291–95] and [the Amir] Tekanā.

[*Rashīd al-Dīn records that Charik (Chärig) the Mongol who had been Qonghurtai's amir-ordu had been dispatched in pursuit of Ahmad with 400 horsemen and behind him another 400 cavalry led by Doladai (Ṫulāī ?) Yarghūchī and that later, on Tuesday 25th Rabī^c II 683/11th July 1284, the other princes and amirs followed though Gaykhatu (r.1291–95) is not mentioned. See pp. 1144–46.*]

Page 65

A messenger named Burah was sent to the Qara'unas who were in Suyur laq (*Siyah Kuh*) to inform them that Ahmad had fled. His message said simply, "You should go and plunder the ordus."

The Qara'unas came to the ordu of Qutui Khātūn where they found Ahmad. They plundered the ordu and ordered Ahmad to be handed over to

60 I must thank Peter Jackson for his careful examination of the original script in Shīrāzī's far from clear hand. The ageing, senior commander Shiktür would have earned the title Āghā by this stage.

them. Sekat (Shiktūr Āghā) and Qarā Noqāī [**38b**] refused to surrender him and told the invaders, "We will guard him together until Arghun comes."[61]

[*Rashīd al-Dīn reports Börä was the shaḥna of Isfahan who the amirs had sent to contact the Qara'unas after the assassination of Alinaq. Börä had been instructed to request them to hunt down and seize Ahmad. Rashīd al-Dīn claims that the Qara'unas overran Qutui Khatun's ordu after she had surrendered Ahmad to the neutral custody of Shiktur Noyan and that they had thoroughly trashed the ordu and grossly humiliated the three khwatin, Qutui, Armini, and Tödäi before placing a guard of 2000 men over Ahmad pp. 1146–47.*]

After that, the talks continued in Tūrghāj where the assembly (*shūr*[62]) deliberated over who should be king. Buqa Āghā said Abaqa had bequeathed the throne to Arghun: "After me Arghun will be king." And Dankiz Küregen attested to this since in the Mongol *yasa* there is no clear ruling on imperial bequests [*hīch beh jāī vasiyyat nīstand*]. Also, Arghun was liked by both the great lords and the army of the Qara'unas, so they agreed upon that.

[*In Rashīd al-Dīn, Abaqa Khan is quoted as saying, "after me Mongke Temur will be king and after him Arghun will be king" p. 1145.*]

On Tuesday 24th Jumādī al-Aval 683 (8th August 1284), Ahmad was tried for the killing of Qonghartai, and he had no excuse for that deed. On the night of Wednesday, 25th Jumādī al-Aval (9th August 1284) they killed Ahmad, in the same way that Ahmad had killed Qonghartai.

On Friday, 27th Jumādī al-Aval (10th August 1284), the king of the world, Arghun, was seated on the throne with celebration in Ṭāla' Qūs (Sagittarius), may it be happy and auspicious for mortals; may his reign increase and his sovereignty be multiplied, with Muḥammad and his family.

Page 66

The night is pregnant, let's see what it gives birth to
Let us wait and see what the finger of the time will touch.
We have seen whatever has come out of the rotation of the sky
And if we live long enough we will see whatever will happen in the future. [**39a**]

61 Waṣṣāf records Shiktūr [Shīktūr] and Qarā Noghāī seizing Ahmad, p. 136.
62 The meaning, origins, language of this word remains elusive.

List of Personages

Figure BM1.1 Qaraqoyunlu Sheep circa 1450

Standing outside a tiled tomb-tower outside Yerevan, built by the khans of Qaraqoyunlu, this stylised sheep was a symbol of their roots in the steppe. The Aqqoyunlu and the Qaraqoyunlu were the last Chinggisid rulers of Iran.

Photo by author

The following is a list of the names which appear in the *Akhbār*, in the introductory chapter, and in the footnotes. The names are accompanied with a short explanation of who they are, their role in context, and their connection with other players. Unfortunately, there is no universal system of transliteration, nor is there any universal agreement on the spelling of names in the various languages in which the names first appeared and the result is a great deal of confusion. Names frequently have different spellings in the same manuscript, even on the same page. In a bid to lessen this confusion, the following list contains the names as they appear in the *Akhbār*, as they appear in Rashīd al-Dīn, as they commonly appear in other works and also, where it is deemed helpful or interesting, as they appear in scholarly publications with diacriticals. To make matters more confusing, some names appear in different forms within the few pages of the *Akhbār-i-Moghūlān dar Anbāneh-ye Quṭb* itself. However, it is hoped that this list will be self-explanatory.

Abaqa Ilkhan, r.1265–82. The second Ilkhan who has generally been treated well by the sources.

'Abdul-Rahman Rifā'ī, Shaykh Kamīl al-Dīn, a Sufi and close adviser to Sultan Ahmad Tegudar, died in Mamluk prison after leading an envoy to Cairo.[1]

Abukān Noyan, son of Shiremun Noyan, son of Chormaghun, military governor of Iran until 1241.

Āchū Sokarchī, Amir, a Tangqut, hero of battle for Baghdad, [Rashīd al-Dīn, p. 1026].

Afshar, Iraj 1925–2011, giant of Persian studies, professor at Tehran University.

Ahmad see Tegudar

ᶜAlā' al-Dīn Jāstī, Shahna of Damascus appointed by Hulegu.

ᶜAlā' al-Dīn Moḥammad III, Ismā'īlī Imam/Caliph, r.1221–55.

Alfī,[2] al-Malik al-Manṣūr Saif ad-Dīn Qalāʾūn al-Alfi as-Ṣālihī an-Najmī al-ʿAlāʾī, r.1279–90; sold for 1000 dinars in 1240s into household of Sultan al-Kamīl.

A Qipchaq Turk who had also been a slave of the sultans of Syria, namely the family of Salāh al-Dīn.

Alinaq [*ᶜAlīnāq*] Bahadur, son of Tugur (a Tongqayit Kerayit), son-in-law of Ahmad through Kuchuk Khatun.

Altāī Bulaghan [*Bulaghān*] Khatun, wife of Abaqa Khan.

Arghun Aqa (d.1278), the remarkable survivor, Arghun Aqa successfully served his office including governor of Iran, despite various attempts to destroy him and undermine his position.

1 Rashīd al-Dīn, p. 1133.

2 al-Malik al-Manṣūr Saif ad-Dīn Qalāʾūn al-Alfi as-Ṣālihī an-Najmī al-ʿAlāʾī, r.1279–90; sold for 1000 dinars in 1240s into household of Sultan al-Kamīl.

Arghun Khan (r.1284–91), the fourth Ilkhan, son of Abaqa. Though he originally supported the nomination of his uncle, Ahmad Tegudar as Ilkhan, with the widespread support for him he turned against the Ilkhan.

Armini [*Armanī*] Khatun, Onggirat wife of Ahmad.

Ārqān, Abaqa's concubine from the household of Qutui (Qūtī) Khatun.

Aruq/Uruq [*Ārukh*] Āghā, brother of Buqa, two leading amirs in early Ilkhanate.

Aṣīl al-Dīn Zozanī, Khwāja, wazir to the Nizari Caliph in Alamt, Rukn al-Dīn.

Aybak, Mujāhid al-Dīn, d.1258, Lesser Dawātdār to the Caliph of Baghdad, Mustaᶜṣim.

Baba, Hulegu's seventh daughter, Lagzi Kuregen's wife, and the sister of Abaqa Khan.

Baidar [Bāīdar]

Baiju Noyan [Bāyjū Nūᶜīn], appointed successor to Chormaghun 1241 as military governor of Iran, maligned in Mustawfī's *Zafarnama*; publicly criticized by Hulegu, executed circa 1260 by Hulegu.

Balghāī/Bālāqāī; Jochid amir; see Tūtār below. (Balghāī, Tūtār, and Tūlī).

Baśar (Yasar) Oghul, Brother of the Chaghadaid prince, Baraq Khan.

Baybars, Abu al-Futuh, al-Malik al-Ẓāhir Rukn al-Din Baibars al-Bunduqdar (1223–1 July 1277); r.1260–77.

Berke Khan, brother of Batu Khan, ruler of the Golden Horde, Qipchaq Khanate 1257–66; allied with the Mamluks of Cairo and supported Ariq Buqa against Qubilai Khan in the Chinggisid civil war of 1260–64.

Börä, the shaḥna of Isfahan and envoy to the Qara'unas.

Boyle, John Andrew, 1216–78, Orientalist, historian, translator of Juwaynī and Rashīd al-Dīn.

Bulghān, *shaḥna* of Shiraz, supporter of Ahmad.

Buqa, Buqa Āghā, after central role in Arghun Khan's campaign against Ahmad, he dominated the government during first four years of Arghun's reign; son of the Jalayir Ögöläi Qorchi, executed 1289 after prestigious career as vizier then Chingsang under Arghun. He first served under Abaqa with his brother Aruq.

Buqa Temur, Kuregan or son-in-law, son of Chinggis Khan's daughter, Chechegen; Oirat commander in Hulegu's army, one of 'royal princes' listed by Juwayni.

Chaghatai [Jaghatāī] Khan, d.1244/45.

Charīk (Chärig) Temur, son of Tükal Bakshi, (Qonqurtai) Qonghartai's amir-ordu later in the employ of Arghun Khan; executed on Ahmad's orders 8th May 1284.

Chinggisids: the preferred name given to the followers of Chinggis Khan and those involved with the state and empire which he founded. 'Mongols' suggests an ethnic identity whereas the Chinggisids were a multi-cultural, multi-ethnic people from diverse backgrounds and ethnic groups.

Dankiz Küregen [son-in-law], possibly a Tatar regimental commander, the son of Burachu, the son of Dörbäi Noyan, the commander-in-chief of Diyarbekir, the son of Quli Noyan adopted son Tolui's son, Sübügätü.[3]

3 Rashīd al-Dīn, p. 87.

Dokuz [Ṭoghūz] Khatun, d.1265; chief wife of Hulegu Khan.
Doladāī Yarghuchi. (see Ṫulāī Yarghūchī), son of the Arulat, Chaghadai Noyan; he was an amir and a judge who tried Shams al-Dīn Juwaynī.
Gaykhatu [*Geikhātū*], Ilkhan, r.1291–95.
Ghazan [*Qazān*] Ilkhan, r.1295–1304.
Güyük Khan, Qa'an or Great Khan, r.1246–48; married Oghul Qaimish.
Ḥamdallah Mustawfī Qazvīnī, 1281–1349, from a veritable Persian family of government officials, administrator and historian, buried in Qazvin
Ḥasan Mazanderanī, the Alid assassin of Rukn al-Dīn, the Ismā'īlī caliph in 1257.
Howorth, Henry, 1842–1923, historian of the Mongols, "The History of the Mongols" published 1876.
Hülegü [Hūlākū], r.1256–65, first Ilkhan.
Hulechu, son of Hulegu; Huleju, twelfth son of Hulegu, son of concubine in Dokuz Khatun's ordu.
Ishan Mangali, qalandar, confidant and intimate of Sultan Ahmad Tegudar.
'Izz ad-Dīn Kaykāwus II bin Kaykhusraw, r.1246–57; the Saljuq sultan of Rum; died in exile in Crimea 1280.
Jochi [Tūshī] Khan, first born son of Chinggis; question regarding paternity and some thought he was a Merkit bastard; d.1226.
Jalāl al-Dīn, son of the Lesser [Kūchuk] Dawātdār, Aybek; escaped Baghdad and fled to Cairo.
Jalāl al-Dīn Mingburnu Khwārazmshāh [1231]; the last Khwārazmshāh whose reign was spent in exile either fleeing the Chinggisid army or criss-crossing Greater Iran, robbing and plundering at will. He was ambushed, robbed, and murdered by Kurdish bandits who were at first unaware of the prize that they had trapped. Mingburnu or Manguberdi is Turkic for 'Godgiven'. After his death, his army moved south-west and became mercenaries.
Jochids: Ghūnkarān, after him came Shībān Khan, then Batu Khan, then Berke, then Möngke Timur [Monkū Timūr], and then Tuta Mongke [Tūtā Monkū] Shah, 680/1281–82. According to the *Akhbār*.
Jurghudāī, (*Jirqudai*) a Jirqin Kerayit amir of a thousand, brother of Bulughān, the shaḥna of Shiraz.
Jushkab [*Jūshkāb*], son of Jumqur, son of Hulegu; he arrived in Iran with Qutui Khatun just after Hulegu's death. Ahmad had assigned him duties in Baghdad.
Jūzjānī, Minhaj al-Siraj, 1193–1260; he wrote *Tabaqat-i Nasiri* (1260 CE) for Sultan Nasir al-Dīn Mahmud of Delhi.
Juwaynīs, 'Alā' al-Dīn Aṭā Malik, 1226–1283, and Shams al-Dīn Muḥammad the Ṣāḥib Dīvān, c. 1220s – 1285. Their father, Bahā al-Dīn Moḥammad served under Jalāl al-Dīn the Khwārazmshāh before switching allegiance to Ögötei Qa'an and the Chinggisids.
Kāmiliyān, Ayyubids 1171–1260; al-Malik al-Kamil Naser ad-Din Abu al-Ma'ali Muhammad) (c. 1177–1238) the fourth Kurdish Ayyubid sultan of Egypt. Under sultan Kamīl [Meledin], the Ayyubids defeated the Fifth Crusade but as a result of the Sixth Crusade, he ceded Jerusalem to the Franks and is known to have met with Saint Francis.

Ket Buqa Noyan, Hulegu's commander-in-chief, killed at the battle of Ayn Jalūt, 1260; he was a Christian, and former *ba'urchi* (cook) in Tolui Khan's household.

Khwārazmshāh; title taken by the rulers Khwarazm, a region of western Turkistan. The title was used from 1077 to 1231. Originally Samanid, Ghaznavid, and Saljuq vassals or iqtā'dār (iqta-holders) Tekish [d.1200] declared himself fully independent and clashed with the Caliph in Baghdad. His son, ᶜAlā al-Dīn Moḥammad II, famously murdered Chinggis Khan's envoys and died ignominiously in 1220 of pleurisy on the Caspian island of Abaskun.

Khwarshāh [*Khūrshāh*], Title of Ismā'īlī Imam or Caliph, Rukn al-Dīn, 1255–1256.

Kūckak, (küchük) Unuqi executed along with Prince Qonghartai (Qonqurtai) and Sādī (Shadai Aqtachi).

Lagzi [*Lakzī*], Lagzi Gürägän son of the former governor of Iran (1243–55), the Oiyat Amir Arghun Aqa [d.1278]. Lagzi married Hulegu's seventh daughter, Baba. His brother Nawruz [d.1297] married Abaqa's daughter, Toghanchuq, and was instrumental in the conversion of Ghazan Khan [r.1295–1304] to Islam.

Majd al-Dīn ibn Athīr, court official investigating financial affairs of the Juwaynī brothers; he was former deputy under 'Aṭā Malek Juwaynī.

Majd al-Mulk Yazdī, former *na'ib* of Shams al-Dīn Juwaynī, who then conspired to destroy both brothers, protected by Yisübuqa, son of Altachu Aqa; became auditor-general under Abaqa; killed in 1282 after being thrown to the mob and pulled apart on the orders of Ahmad Tegudar.

Malek Nāsir, Sultan al-Malik al-Nasir Salah al-Din Yusuf ibn al-Aziz ibn al-Zahir ibn Salah al-Din Yusuf ibn Ayyub ibn Shazy, Ayyubid Amir of Aleppo, 1236–60.

Mamluks were military slaves often from Turkistan or the Caucasus. Turkish boys were often sold into slavery because they were highly prized for their horsemanship. The Mamluk dynasty of Egypt (1250–1517) is the most famous of the regimes run by the military after coups initiated by Mamluk commanders but others include the Delhi Sultanate (1206–1290), the Ghaznavids (977–1186), and more recently, the Mamluks of Iraq (1704–1831).

Māzūq Āghā [Aqa] Qushchi, son of Qara Yurtchi (Yangi) of the Kürlü'üt, one of Hulegu's commanders.

Möngke Qa'an, Great Khan, brother of Toluid khans, Qubilai, Hulegu, and Ariq Buqa, r.1249–59.

Möngke Timur (1256–82), the son of Uljayi [Ūljā] Khatun, brother of Abaqa.

Moqdam al-Dīn Moḥammad Mobāraz (Mubariz al-Dīn Alī Turan) Ismā'īlī army commander who broke through the siege of Gird Kuh, along with Shuja al-Dīn Hasan Astarabadī.

Mujāhad al-Dīn Bebakaraz, see Aybek, the Lesser Dawātdār.

Mulahida, the heretics or Ismā'īlīs.

Musta'ṣim bil'allah Abū Aḥmad, caliph of Baghdad, r.1242–58.

Mustawfī, professional title for an accountant or financial administrator; most notably the historian, Hamdallāh Mustawfī Qazvīnī [d.1349] from the well-known family of government officials from Qazvin who were rivals and sometime enemies of the Juwaynīs.

Muẓaffer al-Dīn Abū Bakr bin Saᶜd, the Salghurid Atābek of Fārs, r. 1226–1260.

Noghai Yarghuchi [*Nuqāī Yarghūchī*] Noghai Yarghuchi is of the Baya'ut tribe, and he was connected through marriage with the royal family. As a yarghuchi, a judge, he presided over disputes and rifts.

Noyan, pl. noyat; general, though in the plural it is generally used to refer to the military elite and politically powerful who vied for ultimate power with the ruling khan's court.

Ögötei [Hūkatāī] Khan, Qa'an, second Great Khan, r.1229–41.

Ordu Buqa son of Nawruz Aqa d.1297, the son of the Oirat, Arghun Aqa d.1278.

Parvāna, (Perwana, Parvāne) Mu'īn al-Dīn Sulaymān, governor and representative of the Ilkhan in the Saljuq Sultanate of Rum in the capital of Konya, executed for treason in 1277.

Qadān, [Qadaqan] amir; Qadān, the brother of Guyuk Khan r.1246–48 was in the service of Qubilai Khan. References in *Akhbār* either erroneous, possibly unknown associate or son of associate of Shishi Bakhshi such as Sönitäi Noyan or his sons including Emgächin, or the infamous and ambitious Ṫaghājār [Taghachar] Noyan. Rashīd al-Dīn names various possibilities, pp. 1134–48.

Qara Buqa, the son of Altajū Bitigchi,[4] governor of Fars under Abaqa and administrator of his *inju*[5] lands.

Qaramush (Qurumshi), the son of Hindu Āghar (Hinduqur); he was a commander of a thousand, amir-tuman, later implicated in Buqa's plot against Arghun Khan.

Qarā Noqāī, a son of Prince Yoshmut, executed with his brother Sogai for rebellion in 1289.

Qazvīnī, large, extended family of administrators based in the northern Iranian city of Qazvin; sometime rivals of the Juwaynīs.

Qonghartai [*Qonghartāī*], son of Hulegu, in 1284, murdered by Sultan Ahmad Tegudar (r.1282–84).

Quduz, Sultan al-Malik al-Muzaffar Saif ad-Din. Defeated Ket Buqa at Ayn Jalut. Assassinated by Baybars 1260. Claimed descent from Ala al-Din Mohammad Khwarazmshah.

Qurumushi Kuregan, son of the Tongqayit Kerayit, Alinaq Bahardur.Qutlugh Khatun, Arghun's wife,

Qutui Khatun [*Qūtūī, and other similar spellings*], Hulegu's Onggirat wife, mother of Ahmad.

Raverty, Henry George, 1825–1906, Colonel in the British Raj who translated Juzjani's history of the mediaeval eastern Islamic world.

Rukn al-Dīn Ḥasan, Khwarshāh, d.1256, Nizari Ismā'īlī caliph in Alamut.

Rukn al-Dīn Qilij Arslān IV bin Kaykhusraw the sultan of Rum, 1248–65.

Rukn al-Dīn, Abu al-Futuh Bekodesh Bunduqdār **Baybars**, 1223–1 July 1277, a Qipchaq Turk and Mamluk sultan of Egypt.

Rumi, Jalāl al-Dīn [1207–73], cleric, and later a Sufi-poet and founder of the Sufi order of Mevlevi. He was known by the honorific, Maulana. Though not an apologist for the Ilkhans, he advised his disciples to cooperate with

4 A Bitigchi is a high-ranking official or scribe who exercised considerable power in Ilkhanid Iran.

5 Inju, enchu, are crown lands, personal estates of the sovereign.

the Ilkhanid authorities and acted as an adviser to the Parvāna Mu'īn al-Dīn Sulaymān.

Sādī (Shadai Aqtachi), amir, aide to Prince Qonghartai (Qongqurtai), executed with Küchük Unuqchi 1284.

Sakat Āghā, possibly Qarā Noqāī's, brother Sogai, both sons of Yoshmūt but a more likely explanation is Shiktür Noyan, the elder statesman, military commander, and viceroy; Shiktür Noyan was the second son of the legendary general, Elgäi Noyan. Waṣṣāf reports an episode towards the end of Ahmad's reign when the two act conjointly (Waṣṣāf, p. 136; *Tahrir*, p. 80).[6]

Shāhanshāh, brother of Rukn al-Dīn Hasan Khwarshāh (Khurshah), d.1256, of Alamut Castle.

Shahneh, A Shahneh in Persian, a Basqaq in Turkish, and a Daraghuchi in Mongolian, and roughly interchangeable terms meaning an overseer or representative of the imperial power, appointed by the Khan to whom he would report back and whose interests he would protect.

Shams al-Dīn Qomī, Qāḍī, a Shi'ite religious judge, and government overseer of Damascus appointed by Hulegu.

Shāżī (Shadai), the son of the great Suqunjaq Noyan, husband of Orghudaq.

Shīrānshāh, another brother of the Ismā'īlī caliph Rukn al-Dīn Hasan Khwarshāh (Khurshah) to delay the final submission of Alamut.

Shishi Bakhshi [*Shīshī Bakhshī*], the Grand Amir, loyal to Arghun; crucial in the deliberations over the succession crisis; the Ilkhan Ghazan's Khitan tutor; guardian of Arghun Khan's *aghruq* (camp for commanders' domestic charges during battle).

Sogai [*Sūkā*] son of prince Yoshmut, executed for treason against Arghun Khan in 1289.

Suqunjaq Noyan [Sūnjāq Nūᶜīn, Sughunchaq, Su'unchaq Aqa], Ilkhanid viceroy, son of Sodun Noyan of the Soldus, and commander of the right hand of Hulegu's forces, captain of the guard under Kökä Elgä.

Tabshīn, brother of Abaqa, sixth son born of Noqachin, the mother of Yoshmūt; had son named Sati.

Taghai Temur [*Ṭaghā Timūr*], fourteenth son of Hulegu, of concubine mother from Qutui's ordu, two sons, Qurumshi and Hajj.

Ṫaghājār [Taghachar] Noyan, d.1296; of the Suquai'ud branch of the Baarin clan; Ilkhanid amir associated with court intrigues during Arghun's years and especially for his part in the bloody elimination of the Jewish wazir, Sa'd al-Dawlah (r.1289–91), and the progrom against the influential Jewish community of the early Ilkhanate.

Takeshī[n][7]/Takshin, fourth son of Hulegu, father of Tobun.

Tekanā (Teknā, Tekana, Tägänä), Great Amir Tägänä Totqavul, general under Abaqa, governor of Khorasan; *totqavul* means highway patrol.

6 I must thank Peter Jackson for uncovering this connection.

7 Not to be confused with Prince Takshī was the son of Böchök, half-brother of Hulegu.

Tegudar, Sultan Ahmad (Tekūdār), 3rd Ilkhan r.1282–84.

Ṭījū (Jitu?) and Taknā (Täknä), sons of Shiktür Noyan, the second son of Elgäi Noyan, Hulegu Khan's greatest general; because of the confusion caused by careless copyists some references to T, K, N, Ā, might have referred to these men.

Tolui [Tūlī] Khan, d.1232; youngest son of Chinggis and Borte.

Toqiyatai (Tuqtani) Khatun, Kerayit daughter of Abaqu; wife awarded Qonghartai by his brother, Ahmad, before dispatching him to Anatolia; she was in the camp of Dokuz Khatun and was the daughter of one of Ong Khan's sisters.

Tubat/Tobun who was the nephew of Ahmad and the son of Takshin, Hulegu's fourth son.

Tūdavān bin Sodūn, (Tödä'ün Bahadur), Suqunjaq Noyan's brother and grandfather of the Amir Chupan; joint military commander of Anatolia with Tūqū, son of Sodun Noyan of the Soldus.

Ṫulāī [Doladai] Yarghūchī, see previously.

Tūlī, Jochid amir; see Tūtār as follows.

Tuq Temūr Keregan, the son of Abdallah Āghā (general of Abaqa), married to Eshil, daughter of Hulegu's fifth son Taraghai.

Tūqū bin Elkāī, (Tughu Bitigchi), Elgäi Noyan's son, military commander in Anatolia with Tūdavān.

Tutāī Khatun (Tödäi), concubine of Abaqa, briefly married to Ahmad, and finally married to Arghun; Mustawfi claims that Ahmad's passion for Tutāī Khatun led to his downfall.[8]

Tūtār, one of three Jochid princes seized by Hulegu on sedition charges [*Rashīd al-Dīn has Bulughā(n), Tūtār and Qulī, p. 1044*], Balghāī, Tūtār, and Tūlī.

Ṫutāq (Taitaq), an amir of a thousand, son of Qubai Noyan was Abaqa Khan's kükältash (foster-brother), and Ahmad's amir-ordu; Shīrāzī erroneously reports his execution.

ᶜUmar, Omar, Prince (Oghul), the son of Sultan Ahmad Tegudar , r.1282–84.

Ward, Leonard J., his 1983 PhD dissertation included a translation of the last section of Mustawfī's verse chronicle. This section dealt with the Ilkhanate up until the final years of Abū Sa'īd's reign.

Yoshmūt, third son of Hulegu and Noqachin Egächi "of the Cathaian bone"; Noqachin was a concubine in Qutui Khatn's ordu.

Yarghūchī, title denoting profession as a presiding judge at a yarghūchī secular court hearing.

Yula Timur [*Yūlā Tāmūr and Yūlā Timūr*]; he is called Ulai Temür in Rashīd al-Dīn. Yūlā Tāmūr's son, Baqā'ī, was one of Mustawfī's informants.

8 Mustawfī, tr. Ward, *Zafarnama*, vol. 2, p. 294.

Figure BM1.2 Yurt, Ulun Baatar Airport

A mobile, embroidered yurt in which the original Mongol khans lived and travelled across the expanses of Asia.

Photo by author

Bibliography

al-ᶜAflakī ᶜĀrifī, Shams al-Dīn Ahmad, *Manāqib al-ᶜārifīn*, ed. Tahsin Yazici, vol. 1 (Ankara: Turk Tarih Karumu Basimevi, 1959); Shams al-Dīn Ahmad ᶜAflākī, John O'Kane (tr.), *The Feats of the Knowers of God* (Leiden and Boston: Brill, 2002).

Aḥārī, Abu Bakr Qoṭbī, *Tārīḵh-i Shayḵh Ovays*, ed. and tr. J.B. Van Loon (The Hague: Mouton & Co., 1954); *Tavārīkh-i-Shayḵh Ovays*, ed. Iraj Afshār (Tabriz: Intashārāt Sotudeh, 2010).

Akasoy, Anna Ayse, and Charles Burnett, *Rashid Al-Din: Agent and Mediator of Cultural Exchanges in Ilkhanid Iran* (London: Warburg Institute Colloquia, 2013).

Allsen, Thomas, *Culture and Conquest in Mongol Eurasia* (Cambridge: Cambridge University Press, 2001).

Amitai, Reuven, and Michal Biran, *Mongols, Turks, and Others: Eurasian Nomads and the Sedentary World* (Leiden and Boston: Brill, 2012).

Amitai, Reuven, and Michal Biran, *Nomads as Agents of Cultural Change: The Mongols and Their Eurasian Predecessors* (Hawaii: University of Hawaii Press, 2015).

Āmulī, Maulānā Awliyā' Allāh, *Tārīkh-i-Rūyān*, ed. Minūchichr Sutūda (Tehran: Inteshārāt Baniyād va Farsang, 1969/1348).

Arberry, A.J., *Shiraz: Persian City of Saints and Poets* (Norman: University of Oklahoma Press, 1960).

Bar Hebraeus, E.A. Wallis Budge (tr.), *The Chronography of Gregory Ab'l Faraj the Son of Aaron Hebrew Physician Commonly Known as Bar Hebraeus Being the First Part of His Political History* (Piscataway, NJ: Gorgias Press, 2003). https://archive.org/details/BarHebraeusChronography.

Barthold, W., *Turkestan Down to the Mongol Invasion*, "E.J.W. Gibb Memorial" Series (London: Luzac & Co, 1977).

Bayḍāwī, Naṣīr al-Dīn Abū al-Khair ᶜAbdullah ibn ᶜUmar, *Nizām al-tavārīkh* (Tehran: Hayāt Gozīnesh Ketāb, 2003/1382).

Biran, Michal, "The Battle of Herat (1270): A Case of Inter-Mongol Warfare", in Nicola Di Cosmo (ed.), *Warfare in Inner Asian History* (London and Leiden: Brill, 2002), pp. 175–220.

Biran, Michal, *Chinggis Khan: Maker of the Muslim World* (London: Oneworld, 2007).

Biran, Michal, "Jovayni, Shams al-Din", *Encyclopaedia Iranica.*

Biran, Michal, *The Empire of the Qara Khitai in Eurasian History: Between China and the Islamic World* (Cambridge: Cambridge University Press, 2005).

Biran, Michal, "Music in the Mongol Conquest of Baghdad: Ṣafī al-Dīn Urmawī and the Ilkhanid Circle of Musicians", in Bruno de Nicola and Charles Melville (eds.), *The Mongols and Transformation in the Middle East* (London and Leiden: Brill, 2016).

Bitilīsī, Prince Sharaf al-Dīn, *Sharafnāma or the History of the Kurdish Nation, 1597*, tr. M.R. Izady (Costa Mesa: Mazda Publishers, 2005).

Boyle, John, "The Death of the Last Abbasid Caliph: A Contemporary Muslim Account", ch. 11, in *The Mongol World Empire 1206–1370* (London: Variorum Reprints, 1977).

Bretschneider, Emil, *Mediaeval Researches*, vols. 1 & 2 (New Delhi: Munshiram Manoharlal Pub., 2001), (originally London: Kegan Paul, Trench, Trubner, 1887). www.univie.ac.at/Geschichte/China-Bibliographie/blog/2010/05/20/bretschneider-medieval-researches-1910/.

Browne, E.G., *Literary History of Persia*, 4 vols. (London: T. Fisher Unwin, 1902–1906). http://bahai-library.com/browne_literary_history.

Cambridge Encyclopaedia of Iran: The Saljuq and Mongol Period, vol.5, ed. John Boyle (Cambridge: Cambridge University Press, 1968); online, 2008. https://doi.org/10.1017/CHOL9780521069366.

Cambridge History of Inner Asia: The Chinggisid Age, ed. Nicola Di Cosmo, Allen J. Frank and Peter B. Golden (Cambridge: Cambridge University Press, 2009); online, 2009, 2014. ISBN: 9781139056045. https://doi.org/10.1017/CHO9781139056045.

Cleaves, Francis Woodman, "The Historicity of The Baljuna Covenant", *Harvard Journal of Asiatic Studies*, Vol. 18, No. 3/4 (Dec., 1955), pp. 357–421.

Dānesh-Pajuh, M.T. (ed.), *Tohfa: Nasihat al-Mulūk* (Tehran: B.T.N.K., 1962); unpublished tr. Louise Marlowe from seminar presentation given at SOAS, October 22, 2012; Louise Marlow, Wellesley College, *Uses of Historical akhbār in Some Eleventh-Century Arabic and Persian Mirrors for Princes*.

de Nicola, Bruno, and Charles Melville, *The Mongols and Transformation in the Middle East* (Leiden and Boston: Brill, 2016).

De Rachewiltz, Igor, *The Secret History of the Mongols: A Mongolian Epic Chronicle of the Thirteenth Century*, 2 vols. (Leydan and Boston: Brill, 2006).

DeWeese, Devin, "Stuck in the Throat of Genghis Khan", in Judith Pfeiffer and Sholeh A. Quinn (eds.), *History and Historiography of Post-Mongol Central Asia and the Middle East: Studies in Honor of John E. Woods* (Weisbaden: Harrassowitz, 2006), pp. 23–60. ***a*** .

DeWeese, Devin, "Cultural Transmission and Exchange in the Mongol Empire: Notes from the Biographical Dictionary of Ibn al-Fuwaṭī", in Linda Komaroff (ed.), *Beyond the Legacy of Genghis Khan* (Leiden and Boston: Brill, 2006), pp. 11–29. ***b***.

Elias, Jamal J., *The Throne Carrier of God: The Life and Thought of ᶜAlā al-Dawlah Simnānī* (Albany: State University of New York Press, 1995).

Gilli-Elewy, Hend, "al-Ḥawādiṯ al-ǧāmi'a: A Contemporary Account of the Mongol Conquest of Baghdad, 659/1259", *Arabica*, Vol. 58 (2011), pp. 353–371.

Grigor of Akner, "History of the Nation of Archers", tr. Robert Blake and Richard Frye, *Harvard Journal of Asiatic Studies*, Vol. 3–4 (1949), pp. 269–283; tr. Robert Bedrosian, accessed 6 October 2017. www.attalus.org/armenian/gaint.htm.

Harāvī, Sayf al-Dīn, and Ghulām Riḍā Ṫabāṫāba'ī Majd (eds.), *Tārīkhnāma-ye Herāt* (Tehran: Asāṫīr, 2004–2005/1383).

Hope, Michael, *Power, Politics, and Tradition in the Mongol Empire and the Ilkhanate of Iran* (Oxford: Oxford University Press, 2016).

Ibn al-Athir, *The Chronicle of Ibn al-Athir for the Crusading Period from al-Kamil fi'l-Ta'rikh. Part 3: The Years 589–629/1193–1231: The Ayyubids after Saladin and the Mongol Menace*, tr. D.S. Richards (London: Routledge, 2010).

Ibn Bazzāz, Ghulam Reza Tabataba'i Majd (ed.), *Ṣafwat al-ṣafā'* (Tehran: Intesharat Zariyat, 1994).

Ibn al-Fuwatī, Kamāl al-Dīn ᶜAbd al-Razzāq, *al-Hawȃdith al-Jȃmi'a: Historical Events of the 7th Century AH*, translated from the Arabic by ᶜAbdulmuḥammad Āyatī (Tehran: Society for the Appreciation of Cultural Works and Dignitaries, 2002).

Ibn Ṭabāṭabā al-Fakhrī, *al-Fakhri: On the Systems of Government and the Muslim Dynasties*, tr. C.E.J. Whiting (London: Luzac & Co. Ltd., 1947); Muḥammad 'Alī bin Ṭabāṭabā (Ibn al-Ṭiqṭaqā); M.W. Gulpāygānī (tr.), *Tārīkh-i Fakhrī* (Tehran: Be-negāh Tarjomeh va Nashr Ketāb, AH 1360/ CE 1981); H. Derenbourg (ed.), *Tārīkh al-Fakhrī* (Paris, 1895).

Jackson, Peter, "The Dissolution of the Mongol Empire", *Central Asiatic Journal*, Vol. 22 (Wiesbaden, 1978).

Jackson, Peter, "Mongol Khans and Religious Allegiance", *IRAN*, Vol. 47 (2009).

Jackson, Peter, *The Mongols and the Islamic World: From Conquest to Conversion* (New Haven and London: Yale University Press, 2017).

Juwaynī, Alā al-Dīn 'Atā' Malik, and M. Qazvīnī (eds.), *Tārīkh-i-Jahān Gushā*, vol. 3 (Leiden: Brill, 1958); John Boyle (tr.), *The History of the World Conqueror* (Manchester: Manchester University Press, 1997). http://unesdoc.unesco.org/images/0010/001086/108630Eb.pdf.

Jūzjānī, Minaḥāj ibn Sirāj, *Ṭabakāt-I-Nāṣirī, vol. 2: A General History of the Muhammadan Dynasties of Asia*, tr. H.G. Raverty (New Delhi: Oriental Books Reprint, 1970).

Kamola, Stefan, *Rashid al-Din and the Making of History in Mongol Iran*, PhD dissertation (Seattle: University of Washington, 2013), accessed 28 February 2017. https://digital.lib.washington.edu/researchworks/bitstream/handle/1773/23424/Kamola_washington_0250E_11655.pdf;sequence=1.

Kartlis Tskhovreba: A History of Georgia, ed. Roin Met'reveli and Stephen Jones, tr. Dimtri Gamq'relidze, Medea Abashidze and Arrian Chant'uria (Tbilisi: Artanuji Publishing, 2014). http://science.org.ge/old/books/Kartlis%20cxovreba/Kartlis%20Cxovreba%202012%20Eng.pdf.

al-Kerbelā'ī, Ḥāfeẓ Ḥosayn ibn, *Rauẓāt al-Jenān va Jennāt al-Jenān*, vol. 1 (Tehran: BTNK, 1965/1344).

Khawan, Rene R. (tr.), *The Subtle Rose: The Book of Arabic Wisdom and Guile* (London and Hague: East-West Publications, 1980).

Khwandmīr, Ghiyath al-Dīn, *Tārīkh-i-Ḥabib al-Siyar*, vol. 3 (Tehran: Ketābkhāneh Khayam, 1954/1333); Wheeler Thackston (tr.), *Classical Writings of the Mediaeval Islamic World: Persian Histories of the Mongol Dynasties*, vol. 2: Habibu's-Siyar: The Reign of the Mongol and the Turk Genghis Khan by Khwandamir, tome 3 (London and New York: I.B. Tauris, 2012).

Komaroff, Linda, *Beyond the Legacy of Genghis Khan* (Leiden and Boston: Brill, 2006).

Komaroff, Linda, *Legacy of Genghis Khan: Courtly Art and Culture in Western Asia, 1256–1353* (New Haven, CT: Yale University Press, 2002).

Krawulsky, Dorathea, *The Mongol Ilkhans and Their Vizier Rashīd al-Dīn* (Frankfurt: Peter Lang Pub Inc, 2011).

Lane, George, "Chingiz Khān: Maker of the Islamic World", *Journal of Qur'anic Studies*, Vol. 16, No. 1 (2014), pp. 140–155.

Lane, George, "The Dali Stele", in Nurten Kilic-Schubel and Evrim Binbash (eds.), *Intellectual and Cultural Studies: Feschrift in Honour of Prof. Isenbike Togan* (Istanbul: Ithaki Press, 2012).

Lane, George, *Early Mongol Rule in 13th Century Iran* (London: Routledge, 2003).

Lane, George, "Intellectual Jousting and the Chinggisid Wisdom Bazaar, Festschrift in Honour of David Morgan, ed. Timothy May", *Journal of the Royal Asiatic Society*, Vol. 26, No. 1–2 (2016), pp. 235–247.

Lane, George, "Phoenix Mosque", *Encyclopaedia Iranica*, Last Updated: July 5, 2011, accessed 13 May 2013. www.iranicaonline.org/articles/phoenix-mosque.

Lane, George, "The Phoenix Mosque of Hangzhou", in Bruno de Nicola and Charles Melville (eds.), *The Mongols and Transformation in the Middle East* (London: Brill, 2016), pp. 237–276.

Lane, George, "Sayyed Ajall", *Encyclopaedia Iranica*, Last Updated: June 29, 2011, accessed 14 May 2013. www.iranicaonline.org/articles/sayyed-ajall.

Lane, George, "Tale of Two Cities: The Liberation of Baghdad and Hangzhou and the Rise of the Toluids", *Central Asiatic Journal*, Vol. 56 (2012/13), pp. 103–32.

Lane, George, "Whose Secret Intent?", in Morris Rossabi (ed.), *Eurasian Influences on Yuan China: Cross-Cultural Transmissions in the 13th and 14th Centuries* (Singapore: National University of Singapore Press, 2013).

Lewis, Bernard, *The Assassins: A Radical Sect in Islam* (London: Weidenfeld and Nicolson, 1967).

Masson-Smith Jnr, John, "Hülegü Moves West: High Living and Heartbreak on the Road to Baghdad", in Linda Komaroff (ed.), *Beyond the Legacy of Genghis Khan* (Leiden and Boston: Brill, 2006), pp. 111–134.

Melville, Charles, "Chobanids", *Encyclopaedia Iranica*, Vol. 5, Fasc. 5, pp. 496–502, accessed 28 February 2017. www.iranicaonline.org/articles/chobanids-chupanids-pers.

Melville, Charles, "Ebn Fowatī", *Encyclopaedia Iranica*, Vol. 8, Fasc. 1 (1997), pp. 25–26, accessed 13 May 2013. www.iranicaonline.org/articles/ebn-al-fowati.

Melville, Charles, *The Fall of Amir Chupan and the Decline of the Ilkhanate, 1327–37: A Decade of Discord in Mongol Iran*, Papers on Inner Asia, 30 (Bloomington, IN: Indiana University Research Institute for Inner Asian Studies, 1999).

Melville, Charles, "From Adam to Abaqa: Qādī Baidāwī's Rearrangement of History", *Studia Iranica*, Vol. 30 & 36 (2001/2007), pp. 7–64.

Morgan, David, *Mediaeval Persia 1040–1797* (London: Routledge, 2015).

Morgan, David, *The Mongols* (London: Wiley-Blackwell, 2007).

Morgan, David, and Reuven Amitai, *The Mongol Empire and its Legacy* (Leiden and Boston: Brill, 2000).

Mustawfī Qazvīnī, Hamdullāh, *Ẓafarnāma* (Tehran: Iran University Press, AH 1377/CE 1999), (facsimile of British Library MS Or.2833); L.J. Ward (tr.), *Zafarnamā of Mustawfī*, 3 vols., PhD dissertation (Manchester: Manchester University, 1983).

Mustawfī Qazvīnī, Hamdallāh, and ᶜAbdul al-Ḥusaīn Navāī (eds.), *Tārīkh-i Guzīdah* (Tehran: Inteshārāt Amīr Kabīr, 1983/1362); E.G. Browne (tr.), *The Select History* (London: Luzac & Co., 1913), accessed 27 February 2017. https://archive.org/details/tarkhiguzdao00hamd.

Mustawfī Qazvīnī, Hamdallāh, and Guy Le Strange (tr.), *The Geographical Part of the Nuzhat-al-Qulub*, "E.J.W. Gibb Memorial" Series, 23, (London: Luzac, 1915–1919), accessed 28 February 2017. http://persian.packhum.org/persian/main?url=pf%3Ffile%3D16301012%26ct%3D0.

Pfeiffer Judith (ed.), *Politics, Patronage and the Transmission of Knowledge in 13th–15th Century Tabriz* (Leiden and Boston: Brill, 2014).

Pfeiffer Judith, "A Turgid History of the Mongol Empire in Persia", in Judith Pfeiffer and Manfred Kropp (eds.), *Theoretical Approaches to the Transmission and Edition of Oriental Manuscripts* (Würzburg: Ergon Verlag, 2007), pp. 107–129.

Pfeiffer Judith, and Sholeh A. Quinn, *History and Historiography of Post-Mongol Central Asia and the Middle East: Studies in Honour of John E. Woods* (Weisbaden: Harrassowitz, 2006).

Qāshānī, Abū al-Qāsim, and Mahin Hambly (eds.), *Tārīkh-i Ūljaytū* (Tehran: B.T.N.K., 1969).

Rashīd al-Dīn, Hamadanī, and Wheeler Thackston (tr.), "Rashiduddin Fazlullah Jami 'u' t-Tawarikh: Compendium of Chronicles", in Wheeler Thackston (ed.), *Classical Writings of the Mediaeval Islamic World* (London: I.B. Tauris, 2012). [cross-reference pagination with 1994 Persian edn].

Rashīd al-Dīn, Mohammad Roushan, and Mustafa Mūsavī (eds.), *Jāmaᶜ al-tavārīkh* (Tehran: Nashr Elborz, 1994/1373).

Ratchnevsky, Paul, *Genghis Khan: His Life and Legacy* (London: Wiley-Blackwell, 1993).

Rūmī, Jalāl al-Dīn, *Discourses of Rumi*, tr. A.J. Arberry (London: Routledge, 1995), accessed 27 February 2017. http://rumisite.com/Books/FiheMaFih.pdf.

Saᶜdī, Abū Muḥammad Muṣliḥ al-Dīn b. ᶜAbd Allāh, *Kulliyāt-I Saᶜdī*, ed. Muḥammad-ᶜAlī Furūghī (Tehran: Intesharat-i Qaqanvus, 1984/1363).

Saᶜdī, Muṣliḥ al-Dīn, *Gulistan (Rose Garden)* Saᶜdi: Bilingual English and Persian Edition, ed. and tr. W.M. Thackston (Bethesda, MD: Ibex Publishers, 2008), accessed 27 February 2017. http://sourcebooks.fordham.edu/halsall/basis/sadi-gulistan2.asp.

al-Ṣafadī, Ṣalāḥ al-Dīn Khalīl ibn Aybak, *al-Wāfī bi al-Wafayāt*, vol. 1 (Wiesbaden: F.Steiner, 1981).

Saliba, George, "Horoscopes and Planetary Theory: Ilkhanid Patronage of Astronomers", in Linda Komaroff (ed.), *Beyond the Legacy of Genghis Khan* (Leiden and Boston: Brill, 2006).

Sayili, Aydin, *The Observatory in Islam and Its Place in the General History of the Observatory*, ch. 3 (Istanbul: Turk Tarih Kurumu Basimevi, 1960).

Seyed-Gohrab, A.A. and S. McGlinn, *Safīna-ye Tabrīz: A Treasury from Tabriz: The Great Il-Khanid Compendium* (Amsterdam: Rozenberg Publishers, 2007).

Shabānkarāᶜī, Muḥammad b. ʻAlī, *Majmaᶜ al-ansāb*, ed. Mīr Hāshim Muḥaddith (Tehran: Mu'assasa-yi Intishārāt-i-Amīr Kabīr, 1984/1363).

Shīrāzī, Quṭb al-Dīn, and Īraj Afshār (eds.), *Akhbār-i Mughulān dar Anbāneh-ye Quṭb* (Qum: Library of Ayatollah Mar'ashī, 2010/1431/1389).

Spuler, Bertold (ed.), *History of the Mongols: Based on Eastern and Western Accounts of the Thirteenth and Fourteenth Centuries*, tr. Helga Drummond and Stuart Drummond (New York: Dorset Press, 1968).

Tabrīzī, Abū Majd Muḥammad ibn Mascūd, *Safīneh-ye Tabrīz: A Treasury of Persian Literature and Islamic Philosophy, Mysticism, and Sciences* (Tehran: Iran University Press, 2003).

Thackston, Wheeler M. (ed. and tr.), *Classical Writings of the Mediaeval Islamic World: Persian Histories of the Mongol Dynasties*, 3 vols. (London and New York: I.B. Tauris, 2012).

Tūsī, Naśīr al-Dīn, "The Death of the Last Abbasid Caliph: A Contemporary Muslim Account", ch. 11, in *The Mongol World Empire 1206–1370*, tr. John Boyle (London: Variorum Reprints, 1977).

Waṣṣāf, ᶜAbdullāh b. Faḍlullāh, *Tārīkh-i-Waṣṣāf*, quoted in B. Spuler (ed. and tr.), Helga Drummond & Stuart Drummond (tr. from German), *The History of the Mongols* (New York: Dorset Press, 1968); ᶜAbdullāh b. Faḍlullāh Waṣṣāf Shīrāzī, *Tārīkh-i-Waṣṣāf* (facsimile edition) (Tehran: Ketāb-khāna Ibn Sīnā, 1959).

William of Rubruck, *The Mission of Friar William of Rubruck: His Journey to the Court of the Great Khan Möngke 1253–1255*, tr. Peter Jackson, ed. David Morgan (Cambridge: Hakluyt, 1990).

Index

For Product Safety Concerns and Information please contact our EU
representative GPSR@taylorandfrancis.com
Taylor & Francis Verlag GmbH, Kaufingerstraße 24, 80331 München, Germany

www.ingramcontent.com/pod-product-compliance
Ingram Content Group UK Ltd.
Pitfield, Milton Keynes, MK11 3LW, UK
UKHW021423080625
459435UK00011B/127

* 9 7 8 0 3 6 7 6 0 7 0 4 3 *